ALL THE WRONG NOTES

ALL THE WRONG NOTES

Adventures in Unpopular Music

Dave Hadfield

Scratching Shed Publishing Ltd

First published by Scratching Shed Publishing Ltd in 2013
Registered in England & Wales No. 6588772.
Registered office:
47 Street Lane, Leeds, West Yorkshire. LS8 1AP
www.scratchingshedpublishing.co.uk
ISBN 978-0957559363

A catalogue record for this book is available from the British Library.

Typeset in Warnock Pro Semi Bold and Palatino
Printed and bound in the United Kingdom by
Charlesworth Press, Flanshaw Way, Flanshaw Lane,
Wakefield, WF2 9LP

To my daughter Sophie,
on condition she takes up the flute again.
And to Lea Nicholson and neglected musicians everywhere.

The Author

Dave Hadfield has been a journalist and author for almost 40 years, notably as the rugby league correspondent of *The Independent*. He has also written widely on a range of other subjects. This is his eighth book. He lives in Bolton with his wife, a variable number of children and an alphabetical CD collection.

Contents

Foreword

By Bernard Wrigley

I SEEM to have known Dave Hadfield since God had a train set, and it was a treat to be asked to write some words to preface these witty ramblings.

What I didn't realise, until I read it, was that our paths had crossed previously but neither of us knew.

Dave was at the Dylan concert in 1965 at the Free Trade Hall, and so was I.

I only got there because someone at school couldn't go, and we were right up in the gods, practically in Salford. Had I known that Dave had blagged a royal box then I would have been insanely jealous.

I was at the MacColl concert at the Balmoral, too, and it was after that when Dave (Brooks) & Bernard started the Anchor Folk Club, and Dave (Hadfield) became a regular singer there. Because of that, we tried to open on different nights but he always found out (!).

It's fascinating to see the musical troughs and peaks I experienced reported from a different angle. It may have happened largely in the North West, but change the names and the venues to reveal a nation's reaction to the changes of that most influential decade - the Sixties.

It wasn't the ideal decade in some instances - civil unrest and architecture to name two - but for music and the arts it was astonishing.

I often notice a tinge of jealousy when younger people say 'Oh, did you really see that?' or 'Were you really around then?'

But it doesn't matter which decade shines as your personal teenage year, for this book doesn't dwell there - it carries through to today.

What is evident is that a reader from any era will enjoy Dave's ramblings through his musical influences.

I, for one, certainly did!

Bernard Wrigley, October 2013

Introduction

WHENEVER someone tells me that they are going to see Robbie Williams, Bruce Springsteen or U2 at the 02, Old Trafford or the Sydney Olympic Stadium, I thank my lucky stars that most of the music I love is performed in venues about the same size as a burger bar or a gents' urinal at one of those destinations - and often in a similar state of repair. Some of the best gigs I've ever seen could have been accommodated comfortably, if not in a telephone box or a broom cupboard, then in an average social sitting room.

This, of course, is a generalisation. There are folk festivals with packed marquees and sold-out tours in big auditoria. I've even seen Bob Dylan at the Manchester Arena; or rather, I've seen a dot on the horizon that could equally well have been someone pretending to be Bob Dylan, but who hadn't quite learned the songs.

But, for me, it all began in the upstairs room of a street-corner pub and it will probably finish there. The sort of place where you can be hit by a plectrum, if the artiste loses control of it, as Tom Gilfellon of the High Level Ranters did at one gig, leaving me with a small scar just above the bridge of my nose. Stick that in your mosh-pit.

For someone whose other great interest in life is rugby league, folk music was a perverse, even masochistic choice - a double guarantee of a lifetime of low-level piss-taking from the unenlightened.

'Here he comes....Eh oop, hey nonny nonny, gerrem onside!' If they don't get you with one, they get you with the other. Bizarrely, this applies even to people who secretly rather like folk music.

I recall a mate of mine - a rugby mate as it happens - taking the mick out of my choice of listening for a long journey, only for me to discover on a rummage through the glove compartment that he had the same CD. Only folk music gives you this invitation, almost obligation, to take the piss out of yourself and your lamentable taste. You might almost say that it is part of the tradition.

But what is it that we are mocking? Well, I could give you an academic definition, all about the folk process and the way a song or tune passes through a series of hands, every time being re-shaped, subtly or radically, to meet the needs of performer and audience.

Or I could direct you to the words of Louis Armstrong, who is supposed to have opined that 'all music is folk music. Leastways, I ain't never heard no horse make it.' There was a brilliant concertina player called Lea Nicholson who was on the club scene when I started to become immersed in it. He even made an LP called *Horsemusic* as a nod to ol' Satchmo and a vote for the eclectic view. He played traditional tunes, but he also played the 'Brandenburg Concerto' on multi-tracked squeeze-boxes, as well as pop hits of the day like

'Those Were the Days,' 'Goodbye Blackberry Way' and 'I'm the Urban Spaceman' - which was on the album. Did he cease to be a folk musician when he moved from one genre to the other? I last saw Lea Nick busking in Bolton town centre a few years ago. He was not in great shape, his fingers didn't dance over the buttons as they used to, but rather staggered, and I didn't have the heart to strike up a conversation as I dropped a quid into his hat, but what he was playing was still unmistakeably *Horsemusic*.

Lea played with Mike Oldfield (of *Tubular Bells* fame,) Richard Thompson, Russ Ballard and the BBC Symphony Orchestra, when they needed 14 bars of concertina for a piece by William Walton. He had a minor hit in France with a song called 'Lazy Afternoon' - his quinze minutes of fame. He was the Eric Clapton of the English concertina - not to be confused with the Anglo concertina, which is different - and yet here he is, sitting in the rain outside The Pound Shop, trying to raise enough money for a pint of rough cider in the Man and Scythe.

Wherever he is now, I would like to dedicate this book to him, as well as to all the other singers and musicians who have hit the right note with me over what is now almost 50 years. Your music has been a constant source of delight and I hope my highly-personal reflections upon it have not been too discordant.

For the title itself, however, I am indebted to those two renowned folk musicians, André Previn and Eric Morecambe. If you have ever watched the television at Christmas, you will have seen the famous Morecambe and Wise sketch in which a dinner-jacketed Eric plays the piano abominably. 'Stop it, stop it,' begs the conductor they called Andrew Preview. 'You're playing ALL the wrong notes.'

Eric eye-balls Preview.

'I'm playing all the *right* notes,' he says, very slowly. 'But not necessarily in the right order.'

As for 'Adventures in Unpopular Music,' I have to thank Tony Hannan, because I ran that secondary title past him and he was unaccountably enthused by the prospect of Scratching Shed publishing a book with that on the cover. I need to thank Tony for more than that, because he has been badgering me for years to write a book about music. Anything to stop me burbling on interminably about rugby league, I suppose. A loud chorus of approval too to the Caplans, Ros and Phil, who helped to make it happen.

How unpopular is unpopular music?

Well, the irony is that, from time to time and in various settings, it isn't unpopular at all. That presents a problem, because when it is commercially successful it is usually via something pretty weak and watery. (Insert most recent examples here. Oh, alright then, Mumford and Sons). Even the best stuff can lose its edge when it gets sucked into the mainstream. So we want it to be popular - as in available to and respected by all - but not popular as in being on Radio One and in *Hello!* magazine all the time. It's a tricky balancing act and it's no wonder that those who attempt it frequently fall over. And who am I to have opinions on all this? Nobody at all, apart from someone who has kept his eyes and ears open and, I hope, most of the time his mind open as well.

A Musical Education

IT will not surprise anyone who has heard the hard-to-obtain bootleg recording of me trying to sing 'The Rambling Sailor' to learn that I do not really come of musical stock. I recall my grandma rehearsing Handel's 'Messiah,' but I don't think she was one of the stars of the Zion Methodist Chapel choir in New Mills.

My granddad died when I was six or seven, but one of the few memories I have of him, apart from his ability to paint in oils with both hands simultaneously, is his singing 'Goodnight Irene,' the Leadbelly ditty that ranks as an early roots-crossover 'world music' hit. It was Leadbelly's in the sense that he popularised it. He didn't write it. It's a folk song; nobody wrote it.

The other thing I recall was that my granddad must have been the most sun-tanned white man who ever lived. He was the colour of an old brown boot and could have passed for a delta bluesman, even if the delta was the River

Goyt, on the Derbyshire-Cheshire border, rather than the Mississippi. He didn't get that way from picking cotton, of course, but from tending his roses in the searing heat of a Peak District summer. It wasn't an orange, David Dickinson, sun-lamp tan, either; it was one that spoke of hardly being indoors from March to November.

Appearances aside, he was vaguely entitled to have the blues, as he lost his job and all his money in the cotton slump of the 1930s. Had I but known it, though, he was introducing me to one of the perennial issues of folk music, the process of cleaning it up. In its raw form 'Goodnight Irene' or 'Irene Goodnight' is a pretty raunchy piece of work. For one thing, Irene seems to be under-age and Leadbelly, who would have been old enough to be, well, her grandfather, sings with undisguised lust: 'I'll get you in my dreams.' The bowdlerised version substitutes the more wistful and innocent 'I'll see you in my dreams.' I honestly can't remember which version Alf Houghton sang as he went about his carpentry, his painting and his rose-growing in New Mills, but it is likely to have been the cleaned-up one taken into the charts by The Weavers in 1950. Others to cover it include Frank Sinatra, Jerry Lee Lewis, Johnny Cash and - by far the best for my money - Ry Cooder with the Tex-Mex accordion player, Flaco Jimenez.

'Goodnight Irene' is also the fans' song at Bristol Rovers, first coined as 'Goodnight Argyle' during a particularly satisfying win over Plymouth. It's the folk process in action, but I'm fairly confident he didn't get it from them.

His daughter, my mother, developed some very strange musical tastes in later life - of which more anon. My dad, whose parents I never knew, has a very orderly approach to music. He has one CD of *Classical Favourites* which he plays every morning at the same time. He knows when he hears 'The Lark Ascending,' for instance, that his first brew of the day should be ready. Music is okay, but strictly in its time and place - and not too loud.

Compared with his younger self, my dad, at 98, is a bit of an old hippy. When I think back to my childhood, a big slice of it spent on the western fringes of London, though, it's clear that my folks, like a lot of parents, were doing their best to fight a rearguard action against the steady advance of popular and youth culture; jeans, chewing gum, rock'n'roll and all that American rubbish.

We didn't have a telly and I think I must have been pretty culturally sheltered in our maisonette above the baker's shop. My pal, Gordon Edwards, who lived at the end of the crescent of shops, above the chippy that was the family business, was a lot more worldly. He showed me a life-sized photo of Elvis Presley, eating chips or drinking 7-Up on an advertising poster. 'Do you know who that is?' he asked me. 'Your brother?' I guessed. Another mate went one better. He had a giant photo of a bikini-clad Brigitte Bardot, assembled from several issues of the newspaper. 'Your sister?' I suggested hopefully. Sadly not.

My other merry memory of life in Hayes, Middlesex, is of my class-mates' attempt at ethnic cleansing. Because I couldn't or wouldn't say barth or parth and insisted on sticking to bath and path, they surrounded me in one PE lesson and bombarded me with bean-bags. It's not exactly being stoned to death by the Taliban, but, whilst one bean-bag is a useful aid to hand-eye co-ordination, forty at the same time are a little hard to handle. Apart from my unacceptable Northernness, I apparently had an annoying Gloucestershire inflexion, because the search for a bakery that wasn't going to shut down took us there for a year as well.

All the Wrong Notes

I was sorry when I was told that my granddad had died, but not sorry when it meant that we had to go back to the North to keep an eye on grandma. Bolton was as close as we could get and that was where I went to secondary school.

We had two music teachers and one of them was as deaf as a post. Ask Tom Berry if you could leave the classroom for any reason and he was likely to reply 'half past ten,' because he thought you had asked him the time. During what was loosely termed singing practice, he would stalk the room, sticking his big, hairy ear about three inches from some bellowing child's mouth. He would listen intently and then shake his head sadly at the pupil's continuing inability to produce any sound whatever.

Some years later, he was knocked down crossing to the pub near his home by something slow and noisy, like a steamroller or a Second World War tank. He never heard it coming.

Despite his deficiencies and difficulties, Tom was very much Good Cop in the music department. Enthusiastically playing the role of Bad Cop was a sadist of the old school whose name I will not dignify in print. Cop that, Maurice Garswood, wherever you are.

There was nothing wrong with his hearing and he could knock out a tune on the piano, but the instrument on which he was a virtuoso was the blackboard rubber. For the benefit of anyone under forty, a blackboard was what teachers used to chalk upon. A blackboard rubber was - hands up anyone who's guessed - what they used to rub it off. A brick-shaped object, about the weight of a cricket ball, it had, like the music department, a hard and a soft side. The soft was some sort of fabric for cleaning the board; the hard was the solid wood by which you held it.

There is a story from the epic years of English football

that Stanley Matthews was so skilful at crossing the ball for the likes of Tommy Lawton and Nat Lofthouse - both of whom went to the school just down the road from mine - that he could arrange it so that the laces pointed away from the centre-forward's forehead. Maurice Garswood had precisely the opposite skill. If he heard something that displeased him - and it could be almost anything: someone singing too loud, too quiet, in the wrong accent, talking, sneezing, coughing, breathing - he would spin around like a dervish and hurl his projectile. It was always the wooden side that connected. You would be drummed out of the profession these days for merely thinking of such a thing. I don't think that happened to him; he was probably ennobled for services to music and education. There was something of the night about Maurice Garswood. In the academic robe he invariably wore, he resembled a malevolent bat and it would have been no surprise to come into the classroom and find him hanging upside down from the ceiling, a board-rubber in his claw.

Perhaps understandably, I didn't learn much in the way of musical theory and I also developed a deep mistrust of classical music; if I stumble across something that I like, the chances are that it has some folk music in its DNA. His lessons did undeniably sharpen my reflexes, though. To this day, I can't [illegible] without instinctively diving for cover. My ignorance of the technicalities and complete lack of grasp of the practicalities of music have, however, put me at a serious disadvantage with the family that has coalesced around me since those days. At the last count, my wife, at least two daughters, a son-in-law and two granddaughters are all equally capable of hearing a new piece of music and immediately knocking out an approximation of it on the old, out of tune piano in the hall. I say out of tune because everyone tells me it is. It sounds fine to me, although I might be influenced by the sure and certain knowledge that it would be me paying several times what I'd spent on the piano to the blind person who would come and retune it. Between them, they can also have a bash at a dazzling variety of other instruments. My youngest has even been known to play an ocarina and nobody knows what one of those is. Needless to say, I'm full of awe and admiration for their accomplishment, mingled with annoyance at their nonchalance. Put them behind enemy lines when the board-rubbers are flying, on the other hand, and they whimper like babies.

But how did I allow this situation to develop? I'm the one who's supposed to be so all-fired keen on music. How come I can't actually DO any? I submit Exhibit A - hands like bunches of pink bananas; okay, on a good day, for catching a rugby ball and for two-fingered tapping on the typewriter or lap-top, but not for much else.

I've tried. I had a bash at the harmonica during my Bob Dylan phase, but rather than plaintive notes summoned up as if from a railroad box-car or from Death Row, I just produced a lot of spittle.

I once owned a five-string banjo - a notoriously temperamental instrument in the best of hands - or rather had one on trial. I tried for a few hours to get a half-decent plunk out of it, then leaned it up in the corner for three weeks. And when I picked it up again, as if by magic, I still couldn't play it. I had a gimbri, a bowed or plucked North African thingumijig, which I bought from the souk in Marrakesh during my Incredible String Band period. Not only was it unplayable, but the goatskin with which it was covered rotted, making mine even smellier than the average teenage bedroom.

It is no wonder, then, that I am not only full of

wonderment at what a Bert Jansch, a Barney McKenna or a Dave Swarbrick can coax from a stringed instrument, I'm also pretty impressed by my six-year-old grandson strumming his plastic ukulele.

If you come into our house and hear a few plaintive chords from the back room, it will probably be my son-in-law experiencing the blues on his latest, steel-fronted job. It certainly won't be me. What that has meant is that my love affair with the music has remained essentially unrequited. Given what so many of the songs involved are about, that does not seem inappropriate.

Besides, I did eventually have singing lessons of a very specific type; but that is a different story - and rather a rambling one.

And the Beat Goes Off

IN terms of popular music, I would take a lot of convincing that there has been a better year to be born than 1951.

That makes you old enough to have been vaguely aware that there were things called rock'n'roll and skiffle before The Beatles came along and changed the rules. It makes you the right age to have felt the maximum buzz of excitement from their early singles and the different, darker thrill of The Rolling Stones. It makes you 16 in the Summer of Love. It makes you old enough to have come through all that and moved on to something else by the time The Beatles and The Stones disappeared up their own legends.

The choice of a group to follow in the Sixties was no laughing matter, because it defined how far along the rebellion spectrum you were. When The Beatles became too cosy, there, lurking around the corner, were their evil twins, The Stones. People talk now as though the implosion of The Beatles after a few short years was a disaster that deprived us of who-knows-what treasures. I'd argue that it saved them. In their relevant years, Lennon and McCartney dovetailed their very different approaches into something that had a tense, dynamic life of its own. Compare that with the Lennon of 'Imagine' - as sanctimonious a dirge as 'God Save the Queen' but treated with rather more reverence - and the McCartney of Wings. We don't know what horrors they could have perpetrated together. But we can imagine.

The Beatles - or rather The Quarrymen, as they were originally - started as a skiffle group, part of the first great wave of do-it-yourself pop music. Punk was the second and Rap the third; what they have in common was that you didn't need to be able to play very well - or even at all. I remember being told that I needed to see The Pogues before they learnt to play - before artifice overtook attitude - and I partly see the point.

The Stones, on the other hand, were Rhythm'n'Blues, which, needless to say, had nothing in common with the product peddled under that name today. The word up in lights was Blues. They got their name from a Muddy Waters song and worked hard at doing what young white boys have always done in this genre - trying to sound like old black men. They did a pretty good job of it, but they lost a key element when Brian Jones drowned at the bottom of his swimming pool, even though they had kicked him out of the band a month earlier because of his drug dependency. Jones was a mess, his creative personality wrecked by his gargantuan consumption; according to one girl-friend, what he really enjoyed was dressing up in her clothes.

He was also the world-music influence within The Stones, playing a wide variety of esoteric instruments and hanging out with traditional musicians in Morocco; I'd bet on him having a gimbri from Marrakesh. Without him, the

Stones made an early decision to become their own tribute band. And very nicely they do out of it too.

If the Stones were a little too mild to reliably outrage your parents, there was always The Pretty Things - called after a Bo Diddley song - upon whom you could settle your allegiance. They had hair down to the floor and made Mick Jagger look like a junior bank clerk (although Keith Richards admittedly looked more wasted then than he does now). I noticed the other week that they were embarking on their 50th anniversary tour.

A popular turn around Bolton in the mid-Sixties were the Blackpool group originally known as Rev Black and the Rockin' Vicars. I leave you to guess what their on-stage gimmick was. Quite quickly, they defrocked the Rev Black and then re-spelt themselves as the Rockin' Vickers.

Some venues wouldn't book an act whose mere name was an affront to men of the cloth, but calling yourselves after the local aeronautics firm was fine. Among the many members who passed through the band was the artiste later known as Lemmy, of Motörhead fame.

Bigger groups than the RVs came through town at regular intervals. I can remember seeing The Hollies, The Searchers, Gerry and the Pacemakers, Freddie and the Dreamers, Billy J.Kramer and the Dakotas, all at the Odeon on package tours. Usually, they would be second on the bill, behind a major league Yank, like Gene Pitney, Del Shannon or Roy Orbison. I saw Herman's Hermits; not much to brag about now, you might think, but they were fulfilling a booking at Rumworth Labour Club, despite having had their first number one.

I never saw The Beatles. What should have been my seat mysteriously went to someone else. It led to a punch-up in the playground. I won the fight, but lost the ticket. My enemy that day, it turned out, was also the Tonge Moor Ripper, who had been systematically shredding my exercise books after school, possibly because I sounded too southern.

Where it was really happening, though, was the Beachcomber, a warren of dark rooms in an old warehouse, next to the filthy trickle that was the River Croal. If it felt like a precarious set-up, there was good reason for that; the Top Storey, a similar club in the premises opposite, had burnt down in 1961, leaving 19 people dead, some from smoke inhalation, some from jumping out of the windows into the Croal.

That felt like ancient history at the time, but it can only have been three years before I entered its dark doorway for the first time. It was a destination after school, not least because there were girls there from other schools - an intoxicating thought in itself, although it served nothing stronger than frothy coffee.

At night, if you looked vaguely old enough, you could sneak out to the Dog and Partridge for a pint. The object of the exercise, though, was the music, which seemed a bit more cutting-edge than at other venues. It was there that I saw Steam Packet - a super-group in the making, if ever there was one, with a front line of Rod Stewart, Long John Baldry and Julie Driscoll - the St Louis Union and Victor Brox and his Blues Train. A pre-Cream Ginger Baker brought his own band there. I remember him sitting in the doorway, wondering where he could get something to eat. I've heard an interview with him since, in which he admitted he would have been in the throes of heroin addiction around this time, so it might not just have been pie and chips he was craving.

The night of nights, however, was when The Who came to town. Or came to towns, to be strictly accurate; they played a set at the Beachcomber, them piled into a van for the ten mile dash to the Casino in Leigh, played a set there and came back and repeated the operation. And this was The Who of 'My Generation.' They were it. We were wedged in so tight that there was no room for the sweat to run down the walls. It didn't help that half the audience were wearing fur-lined parkas in the middle of summer. The ceiling over the stage was so low - they almost had to bend Long John Baldry double - that Pete Townsend, himself quite tall for a Mod, had to climb down into the crowd to get a good enough swing to smash his guitar - although not so badly that it couldn't be smashed again an hour later in Leigh.

I saw The Who again a few years later, at a mate's college in Coventry. By this time they were huge, but huge in those days meant that we filled a decent sized hall, sitting cross-legged on the wooden floor like primary schoolchildren at assembly. It was supposed to be the last time they were ever going to perform *Tommy*. That didn't quite turn out to be the case - they'll probably still be doing it in their eighties - but it was almost certainly the last time they played it at a polytechnic in Coventry. Of the two shows, I preferred the one at the Beachcomber. Whenever I describe Bellowhead as the best live band I've ever seen, someone will say 'What about The Who?' and I say 'Yes, they were pretty good.'

I was keen on first and last gigs. A gang of us went to Loughbrough for the Bonzo Dog Band's farewell performance - and that really was the end of them. It wasn't as final, though, as Johnny Kidd's last hurrah in Bolton. The leader of Johnny Kidd and the Pirates played 'I'll Never Get Over You' and the rest of his repertoire then wrapped his car around a tree on the ring road.

If I had known then what I know now about the whorehouses on New Orleans, I would have cut to the chase and homed straight in on The Animals. They and particularly the four and a half minutes of 'House of the Rising Sun,' were the portal to a different world.

On compulsory family trips on Sundays, I would take my transistor radio to listen to the top ten and dutifully write it down in an exercise book - one that hadn't been ripped up. When 'Rising Sun' charged into the charts, something different was going on. There was its unconscionable length - these were the day of the two and a half minute singles - and it was obviously about something pretty risqué. You couldn't be sure of what; the lyrics are not very specific. But you knew you were on a different planet from Cliff Richard and Frank Ifield.

The Animals were widely thought at the time to have lifted the song from Bob Dylan's obscure eponymous debut album released two years earlier. In fact, it's a quite different version; for one thing it's sung from a male viewpoint, not a woman, as in Dylan's. The folk have never been too fussed about these things.

The Animals' singer, Eric Burdon, had heard what was to become their version from a singer in a Newcastle pub. The singer was Johnny Handle, of the previously mentioned High Level Ranters. That's the thing about the High Level Ranters; you don't think about them for years and then along come two anecdotes at once.

Whilst we're in Newcastle, let's have a third one. I once had the distressing task of telling the Ranters' man on the Northumbrian pipes, Colin Ross, who was also the curator of the city's Bagpipe Museum, that he was not after all going to appear on the regional news programme that night. I didn't even work for the BBC; I was just passing through and they thought that perhaps the bad tidings would come better from a specialist. He was sitting in reception with a selection of bagpipes of the world around him. I told him the disappointing news and I've rarely seen a man more deflated.

Meanwhile, back in the brothels of Louisiana, The Animals were to enjoy a number one in both Britain and America with a traditional lament about syphilis (probably), gambling (definitely), boozing (undoubtedly) and sewing. They initially thought it would make a set-closer with a difference for their tour with Chuck Berry. (Yes, I saw that one.)

Its instant effect on audiences persuaded them to put it out as a single and they never quite matched it. Somewhere, there must have been an English 'root' version - if I may use that term - probably set in Soho, but I've never heard it. Leadbelly and Woody Guthrie recorded it. You could also check out Nina Simone's brooding performance, but for the 'House of the Rising Sun' that everyone knows, we and The Animals have Johnny Handle to thank.

By the miracle of the internet, I've just watched the original footage of them playing it, neat and tidy in matching grey suits and yellow button-down collared shirts. Only Eric Burdon's Tyne-delta growl and some furious organ-playing from Alan Price hint at a wilder world beyond.

It was a pointer to the cross-fertilisation that could and would take place between folk and pop. The most-played record on the jukebox at the Beachcomber, for instance, for months if not years, was 'Keep on Running' by the Spencer Davis Group. The singer of what still sounds like an absolute classic was Stevie Winwood, who later formed Traffic and recorded 'John Barleycorn Must Die,' a relatively straight take on the ancient traditional song about fertility rituals and boozing. It isn't the best version - Tim Van Eyken's is my current favourite - but it's pretty good, as is Paul Weller's with The Imagined Village. Winwood now lives on his country estate in Gloucestershire, where, among other things, he grows barley.

The Animals didn't, by 1960s standards, look very threatening. They even had rather short hair. This was an issue in our house, because my mum had a fixation with its length and tidiness, which meant that for years it was one long battle. We were as stubborn as each other, but even so we had our moments of self-awareness.

'Who's that on the telly?' she asked one time.

'That's a mass murderer, mother.'

'Well, at least his hair's tidy.'

We were only slightly exaggerating the intransigence of our respective positions on the subject. My mum died when she was considerably younger than I am now. If I could turn the clock back and buy her ten years respite from the cancer that killed her, I would have my head shaved down to the bone, but somehow I don't think that was what she wanted either.

It was all part of a more general obsession with cleanliness. On the one occasion I went on a foreign holiday with my parents, we drove right across a whole country without being able to find a hotel or guest house with a bathroom that met her exacting standards. And where was this cess-pit of a nation, this seething cauldron of germs? Somewhere behind the Iron Curtain? One of the more unsanitary backwaters of North Africa? No, Switzerland, where the very air smells of disinfectant. Thank god she never saw some of the places I stayed in years to come.

One good thing about this era I'm revisiting is that, if you weren't in a group yourself, you knew plenty of people who were. I was surplus to requirements for the Alebelly Blues Band, fronted by the considerable bulk of my second-row partner on the rugby field, Johnny Jackson, and even for its expanded line-up, the Alebelly Big Smooth Sophisticated Blues Band. My best mate was the rhythm guitar-player, Dave Part. He had his own amp and speaker, so he was assured of a gig wherever he went.

When he went to university in London, he formed not one band but two. Or rather, he formed the same band twice, because the same members performed as Darryl C and the C-Men, when they were playing retro rock'n'roll, and Gerald and the Geraniums when they were purveying spoof psychedelia. One night, another guitar-player turned up at rehearsals. Well, Part wasn't having that and he gave him short shrift. Okay, said the guitarist philosophically, he was thinking of forming his own band anyway. He did. He called them Queen and, against all the odds, they proved slightly more durable than Darryl C and the C-Men or Gerald and the Geraniums.

I was at a rugby match a couple of years ago when I heard a shout. 'Dave, it's Darryl,' said a vaguely familiar figure, who, I am reminded, was also Ken Livingstone's agent when he stood successfully as MP for Brent. 'Darryl C! Of the C-Men!' You don't get that sort of greeting very often from Queen when you run into them.

Zimmerframe Clues: Genius or Judas?

THE first time I saw the name of the most important writer of songs of the last half-century written down, it was spelt Bob Dillon.

The confusion was with Marshall Matt Dillon of the TV cowboy drama, *Gunsmoke*. Indeed, Dillon might have initially written it that way himself. I also saw it spelt Bob Dylon, rhyming with nylon, and there was a slight mix-up with Bobby Darin. He was clearly the next big thing, but we early adopters had a bit of trouble with the name and telling us that he had called himself after a Welsh poet didn't help at all. News of him filtered back to England; what few knew was that he had already been here in person - and had filled his boots.

The young Robert Zimmerman resembled nothing as much as a giant sheet of extra-absorbent blotting paper. He played in high school rock'n'roll bands, but really started to soak stuff up thirstily when he got to the University of

Minnesota in Minneapolis. That stuff included traditional folk-songs, black music from the likes of Leadbelly and, most significantly in the short term, almost the entire Woody Guthrie song book. He had not emerged as a writer and nobody in his home state seems to have rated him very highly as a performer, but he was gathering his raw material. Dylan describes his immersion in the folk tradition in his candid and revealing autobiography, *Chronicles (Volume 1)*:

> 'I loved all these ballads right away. They were as romantic as all hell and high above all the romantic popular songs I'd ever heard.....
>
> 'I could rattle off all these songs without comment as if all the wise and poetic words were mine and mine alone. The songs had beautiful melodies and were filled with everyday leading players like barbers and servants, mistresses and soldiers, sailors, farmhands and factory girls - their comings and goings - when they spoke in the songs they entered your life.'

In the liner-notes to *Biograph* (1985) he puts it like this:

> 'The thing about Rock'n'Roll is that, for me anyway, it wasn't enough. There were great catch-phrases and driving pulse rhythms but the songs weren't serious or didn't reflect life in a realistic way. I knew that when I got into folk music it was moving to a serious type of thing. The songs are filled with more despair, more sadness, more triumph, more faith in the supernatural, much deeper feelings.'

In 1961, Dylan dropped out of college and bummed a ride to New York, partly to visit Guthrie, who was dying of Huntington's Disease in hospital in nearby New Jersey. It was not quite the equivalent of being anointed by a medieval king, but there was a distinct sense of the baton being passed.

He also began to play in the clubs and coffee bars of Greenwich Village and made enough of an impact to be signed to record his first LP. *Bob Dylan* included 'House of the Rising Sun' and only two of his own compositions. It sold slowly, but made him something of a celebrity back home in Minnesota. It also led to him being invited to England for the first time, primarily to sing and act in a BBC television play. He also explored London's burgeoning folk club scene and befriended one of its leading young singers - Martin Carthy, a name that will crop up repeatedly as this account meanders on. One of Carthy's favourite memories is of the two hacking an old piano to pieces with a samurai sword to burn it and try to keep warm. From Carthy and other singers, he got the tunes that largely underpinned his next three albums - the ones that made him famous. Taking *Freewheelin'*.... alone, he borrowed the tune to which Carthy sang 'Lord Franklin' for 'Bob Dylan's Dream,' 'Masters of War' was a re-working of 'Nottamun Town,' for which one biography says he paid the American singer, Jean Ritchie, $5,000 in an out-of-court settlement. 'Hard Rain....' is essentially a recasting of 'Lord Randall' and 'Scarborough Fair' he effectively raids twice. On *Freewheelin'*... it becomes 'Girl From the North Country'; On *The Times They Are A-Changing* it becomes, at one further remove, 'Boots of Spanish Leather'.

He wasn't on his own either, because 'Scarborough Fair' proved to be a fly-paper for American visitors. Paul Simon turned it into 'Parsley, Sage, Rosemary and Thyme,' which became world-famous on the soundtrack of *The*

Graduate - but more of him later. A slightly different case was 'No More Auction Block For Me,' a slave song that formed the basis of Dylan's first 'greatest hit' - 'Blowin' in the Wind.'

All the British source material would have been familiar in folk clubs in London and Dylan had the ears and memory of an elephant. None of this amounted to plagiarism - although that is an accusation that has followed him through much of his fifty year (and counting) performing career. What it is, rather, is the folk process in vigorous, accelerated action. Martin Carthy didn't own the melody of 'Lord Franklin' any more than Bob Dylan did - and would never have claimed to.

It is considered good manners, however, that when you lift something very definitely crafted and shaped by another individual you should acknowledge it. On the sleeve notes to *Freewheelin'...* Dylan does. Whether that would have made any difference in the case of 'With God On Our Side' is another question. For that song, he used the tune of 'The Patriot Game,' as sung by Dominic Behan, brother of the bibulous playwright, Brendan. There were threats of court action, until it was pointed out that Behan, who called him 'a plagiarist and a thief,' had himself nicked the tune from an Irish song called 'The Merry Month of May.'

The first Bob Dylan record I owned was the single of 'The Times They are A-Changing' with 'Honey Just Allow Me One More Chance' on the B-side. I went to Harker and Howarth's shop that day with the required 6/8d but without being quite sure what I was going to buy. It was between Dylan, the singer lumbered with the tag of 'The British Dylan' - well, Donovan did wear a similar denim cap and played guitar and harmonica - and the theme music from *Doctor Who*. I've always been grateful that I got that decision right.

> 'Come fathers and mothers throughout all the
> land,
> And don't criticise what you can't understand,
> Your sons and your daughters are beyond your
> command.....'

Sweet music indeed, if you were getting plenty of grief over the state of your hair and your bedroom.

Buying an LP was a bigger commitment; 32 shillings (or £1.60 in new money) - the price at which they seemed to be stuck for a generation - was enough for a good night out and your tram-fare home. Having got this intimidating sum of money together, thanks to a Saturday job selling slippers on the market, however, it had to be *Freewheelin'*.... Everything about it seemed perfect, from the front-cover shot of His Bobness walking down a wintery New York street, arm in arm with his girlfriend, the gorgeous Suze Rotolo, to the scholarly sleeve-notes by Nat Hentoff on the back. In between, apart from the songs already mentioned, there were spell-binding tracks like 'Don't Think Twice, It's Alright' and 'Corrina, Corrina.' I played the thing to death on the family Dansette.

Naturally, the hunger to see this guy in person was strong, but when tickets went on sale for his 1965 show at the Free Trade Hall, they sold out instantly. That was where my Uncle Ro came in. Ro, short for Roland, was the sort of uncle every young man should have, except that he wasn't really an uncle at all. He was my mum's cousin's husband, a relationship for which there is no particular name. He was the first relative to take me to the pub and he used to slip me a ten-bob note when nobody was looking. He was that sort of uncle. He was a stubbly little man, a raffish character, a seaman who had been everywhere and finally weighed anchor working as an inspector in the Environmental Health department at Manchester Town Hall. When he heard about my disappointment, he made it his business to get us two tickets. The Free Trade Hall didn't have to find him a couple, but there might have been a rather nasty health scare there if they hadn't.

Not only did we have seats, we had a little box overlooking the stage and the show was everything I'd hoped it would be - just Dylan, his guitar and harmonica, playing one great song after another. In the half-time interval, Ro disappeared, returning with a couple of whiskies for us - I was almost 14, after all - and a neatly folded piece of paper.

'I thought you might want this,' he said - and there, scrawled diagonally, was Bob Dylan's autograph in blue biro, spelt right and everything. He was always rather vague about how he got it, although he remarked that the Free Trade Hall dressing-rooms needed a good fumigating. I like to think of him breezing his way past security, something for which he had a rare gift, kicking the door open and shouting: 'Environmental Health! Everybody freeze!' I feel sorry for anyone who didn't have an Uncle Ro and anyone who missed Bob Dylan's first tour.

Of course, that wasn't the tour that entered into folk-lore. That was the following year. By 1966, even Ro couldn't get me a ticket, but he did get me some sort of quasi-official pass that admitted me to the very back of the top circle, up with the lighting rig. It was from that eyrie that I saw - and sometimes heard - the most infamous concert in the history of dodgy gigs.

A lot had happened in the intervening 12 months. At the Newport Folk Festival in the summer of 1965, Dylan had scandalised the audience by taking the stage with a rock band, plugging in and turning up the volume. There is a story, possibly apocryphal, of Pete Seeger - already the grand old man of American folk music - trying desperately to saw through the power cables and silence the accursed racket. He failed, but the audience succeeded. After three distorted numbers, they heckled Dylan and his band (precursors of The Band) off the stage. Dylan was persuaded to return on his own and sang 'It's All Over Now, Baby Blue' and 'Mr Tambourine Man' with a borrowed acoustic guitar and harmonica.

The same tensions surfaced on the British tour the following Spring, with heckling and walk-outs from the first date onwards. Manchester was a week into the itinerary, so we should have had some inkling that we were not in for the usual exercise in giving the public what it wants. They got it in the first half, an acoustic set played in reverential silence punctuated by polite applause; at least, that's the way it sounds now on *Live 1966. The 'Royal Albert Hall' Concert.* Those internal quote marks are necessary, because the bootleg tape of the show was mistakenly attributed to London. Part two and disc two were something quite different.

The Free Trade Hall, nowadays converted into a luxury hotel, had some worthy qualities; good acoustics were not among them. I'd been to concerts there where the sound had just disappeared into the rafters. This night, up in the gods, it was just a mess; a muddy soup of noise in which you could occasionally detect a familiar ingredient.

The introduction to the second number, 'She Belongs to Me,' laid out the ground-rules. 'It used to be like that,' says Dylan, pre-figuring a whole future career of messing around with his music. 'Now it goes like this.' The heckling and slow-handclapping started after that song, although from up in the lighting rig it was not very obvious; nothing was, except a very loud noise coming from far down below.

To the committed Dylanologist, which I would never claim to be, one of the fascinations of the man must be the way he constantly resurrects songs from his tombstone-sized back-catalogue and makes them almost unrecognisable. In Manchester in 1966, however, hearing this happen to 'One Too Many Mornings,' for instance, was an affront. It was like buying a painting and the artist coming round to your house and slashing it with your kitchen knife.

Finally, between 'Ballad of a Thin Man' and the closing 'Like a Rolling Stone,' we get the J-Word. 'Judas,' shouts someone down in the stalls - a very special insult to someone who had already invoked that name in his work. 'We were just so disappointed,' said the heckler 20 years later. 'It wasn't the Bob Dylan we were used to listening to.'

Don't let anyone tell you that Dylan's response is impressive as a piece of cut-and-thrust repartee. 'I don't believe you,' he says in an embarrassingly girly lisp; he sounds extremely stoned. 'You're a liar!' The story is that he then turns to his band and barks: 'Play fucking louder,' but for the life of me I can't hear that on the CD.

What I can hear is a roar of approval and a round of applause from the audience for the man who was to become known henceforth as Keith 'Judas' Butler. Just by co-incidence, he was a student at Keele University, the seat of learning to which I gravitated four years later, largely on the strength of enjoying the place at various folk festivals. He had left by then and there was no plaque on the campus.

The other thing I can hear, in a new mix made from the master-tapes, rather than filtered through the Free Trade Hall's architecture, is that a lot of the music is pretty bloody marvellous. The closing number, whether Dylan told his band to 'play fucking louder' or not, is blistering. At the end of it, you can only hear applause, no heckling, no Keith

Butler, who had fled in mortification. 'I was just totally embarrassed when he shouted back,' he said. My old mate, Roy, who I've only just discovered was also there that night, recalls police with dogs clearing the hall, but that I can't confirm.

With even a little hindsight, we shouldn't have been surprised by this turn of events. True, Dylan wanted to be Woody Guthrie, but he also wanted to be Little Richard. He could also be called the Godfather of Rap. There wasn't a name for it at the time, but what else is he doing on 'Subterranean Homesick Blues'? It's either that or re-inventing the talking blues format, in which he did much of his early work; or a bit of each.

I have seen Bob Dylan once since, at the Manchester Arena on what has been called his 'never-ending tour.' It was a double bill with Van Morrison and, in my naivety, I half expected that the two grumpy old growlers might do a spot of jamming together. Not a chance; they performed two completely separate shows and totally ignored each other. From our distant seats, they were the aforementioned dots on the horizon; in fact, from where we were, it could have been Morrison singing Dylan and vice-versa. Assuming for a moment that it was Dylan, though, I remember being bemused by his de-construction of 'Mr Tambourine Man,' before deciding that I rather liked it. And it keeps your backing musicians on their toes when they don't know which song you'll be doing next or which tune you'll be doing it to.

Since then, my relationship with the great man has been conducted exclusively through the medium of the CD. I know there are plenty of Dylan completists out there who have to have everything he has recorded, but I'm not among them. There are people of whom I have the full set, but not Dylan; his output is just too wildly uneven. There are albums

I couldn't live without, like *Freewheelin'...* and his greatest, for my money, *Blood On The Tracks,* but there are others, particularly from periods in his life when he had a bad dose of some religion or other, that I wouldn't allow in the house.

Modern Times, a couple of years ago, was a nice surprise and the *Bootleg* series on Columbia is full of obscure delights. Thinking about what I like and what I don't, it seems to me that what I really prefer are what you might call his 'small' songs; not the epics, freighted down with symbolism and allusion, but the concise, condensed snapshots of songs.

You can have 'Desolation Row' if I can have 'You're Going to Make Me Lonesome When You Go' and 'Buckets of Rain' from *Blood on the Tracks*. I've never heard Dylan sing them live, but Martin Simpson's versions will do me fine. The whole album will do me fine; for one thing, it disproves the lazy assertion that Dylan can't sing. His voice on *Modern Times* might have been described as 'a catarrhal death-rattle,' but it doesn't spoil songs like 'Nettie Moore' or 'Workingman's Blues.' On *Blood on the Tracks,* on the other hand, he sings like a linnet throughout.

Another Dylan album on my shelves is more of a worry. *Good As I Been To You* (1992) was a return to his roots, in that it was made up of covers of other people's songs - not theirs by ownership, but by usage and association. 'Canadee-I-O' is unmistakably Nic Jones' work - although Dylan wisely avoids the breathtaking guitar intro - 'Arthur McBride' is Paul Brady, note for note, apart from a few he can't reach, and 'Jim Jones' is equally close to John Kirkpatrick's version, which he in turn credits to Mick Slocum, of the Australian band, The Bushwackers. There are no acknowledgements anywhere on the Dylan album, despite an insert that is blank apart from what appears to be a photograph of clouds. It would have been good manners to devote a fraction of that space to a nod in the direction of his sources. He took plenty of criticism over this, particularly over Nic Jones, who was studiously ignored midway through a 30-year absence from performing following a near-fatal car crash. You can only wonder how handy a composer's credit would have been in the middle of that.

Even *Modern Times* presents a bit of a problem. Some of the lyrics are undeniably close to the work of the American Civil War poet, Henry Timrod. There are those who believe that this represents a continuous and disreputable thread running through Dylan's career. The most outspoken witness for the prosecution is his fellow-singer-songwriter and one-time pal, Joni Mitchell.

In an interview in 2010, she laid her cards on the table, a little like a character in a Bob Dylan song. 'Bob's not authentic at all,' she said. 'He's a plagiarist and his name and voice are fake. Everything about Bob is a deception.'

Well, she always did have a way with words, but I'm tempted to cry out: 'Hang on a minute. This is the music business, where a degree of self-reinvention is not only permissible, it's damn near mandatory.'

An early Dylan bootleg closes with him reading a poem entitled *Last Thoughts on Woody Guthrie*. In that spirit, I might as well attempt a few last thoughts on Bob Dylan. Like this one. Which would be the greater irony: a) that he can produce a more accurate facsimile of other people's work than he can of his own? Or b) that the most popular performer ever to have the word 'folk' applied to him should be the one to be booed from the stage? I'll leave that for the Dylanologists to sort out; and, yes, there are such specialists in this field of study, just as there are Kremlinologists.

I never expected to be quoting Maureen Lipman in

this book, but when she does her schtick as a Jewish mother she has a phrase about well-qualified sons; they have 'an ology.' Only Mr and Mrs Zimmerman of Hibbing, Minnesota, produced a son who actually IS an ology.

Confessions of a Teenaged Traddy

THE first time I walked through the door of the St George's Hotel, I was pinned to the wall by two fat sisters from the Rossendale Valley. It was not a close encounter with a wildly inaccurate women's darts team; it was my first, fateful visit to a folk club.

The pub has long been demolished, but it used to stand on a corner at the edge of the town centre, just up the street from the shop where I had bought my Bob Dylan records. By the record shop till, there was a hand written note sellotaped to the counter: 'Bolton Folk Club. St George's Hotel. Every Thusday.'

'Aha,' I'm thinking, 'this must be for me.' So next Thursday, there I am. It was, from memory, not the traditional set-up in an upstairs room; it was in the back room of the pub and, as soon as I crossed the threshold, I was transfixed. Jean and Elaine Carruthers were not Joan Baez and Julie Felix, who were what I thought I might find in a folk club. As I was to find out, there were plenty in the clubs trying to be Joan Baez or Julie Felix. The Carruthers sisters were trying to be something different.

They were trying to be The Watersons.

Jean and Elaine were the female half of The Valley Folk, a four-part unaccompanied harmony group who ran the club. Just four voices and nothing else, no guitar, no nothing. I was stunned, I didn't know it was allowed. There was nothing 'authentic' about The Valley Folk. Their style of singing was not handed down from generation to generation in the villages around Rawtenstall and Bacup. It was learned from Watersons LPs. Of course, they weren't as good as The Watersons, but they were still pretty damn good. Two songs and I was hooked for life. There was something about the way they stood in a semi-circle, probably with a couple of them cupping their hands over their ears, bouncing notes off each other, that grabbed me and has never really let go. It was harmony, but not as we knew it. They weren't singing in unison, not the same tune in different pitches; they were singing four subtly different tunes that sometimes converged and intertwined, sometimes went their own separate way for a phrase or two. It was a thrilling noise - and it wasn't even as good as it could get.

The Valley Folk didn't do badly. They made an LP, *All Bells in Paradise*, on the prestigious Topic label. It was a concept album of sorts, consisting entirely of lesser-known carols, and I suspect that the song selection was largely the work of Bert Lloyd, the resident expert at Topic. Left to their own devices, they tended to sing a mixture of Lancashire material and, inevitably, songs learned from The Watersons.

The first time I saw The Watersons, at the Free Trade Hall, I thought that their lead singer, Mike of that ilk, had only got one arm. I was a long way back in the cheapest seats and my eyes weren't much cop, even then. After a couple of songs, he uncoiled the missing limb from behind his back - and cupped his hand over his ear.

We can no longer postpone, I fear, the great Finger in the Ear calumny.

The one thing everyone knows about folk singers is that they stick their fingers in their ears, no doubt to protect themselves from the hideous racket they are inflicting on others. Ho ho. It's a good stick with which to poke and thrash us, but the truth is rather more mundane. As Sophie Parkes writes in *Wayward Daughter*, her biography of Mike's niece, Eliza Carthy, singers of many styles have clapped a paw on their lugs on occasion. It slightly amplifies the voice, especially to yourself. The Bee Gees were particular offenders in the world of mainstream pop music and had the piss taken out of them for it by no less a piss-taker than Kenny Everett. To the hoi-polloi, however, nothing raises the hackles or triggers the mirthless mockery like a bearded man doing it, preferably in an Arran sweater. If he also has a pewter tankard within arm's reach, so much the better.

Returning to the number of Mike Waterson's arms, there was, confusingly, another slightly later a cappella group whose leader really did only have one arm. Dave Brady had lost the other one in a motorcycle crash when he was 17, some years before he founded Swan Arcade. Not only did that not stop him singing, it didn't stop him either from playing the concertina, which he did by clasping one end between his knees, or later becoming the roadie for the Scottish Chamber Orchestra. Brady was a manic performer, with his wild eyes and bushy beard, and his tendency to harangue the audience. Swan Arcade were largely traditional in their repertoire, but thought nothing of throwing in The Kinks' 'Lola' or The Beatles' 'Paperback Writer.' They were good. Almost as good as the Young Tradition, in fact. This was cutting-edge a cappella. Their leader, Peter Bellamy, had the full complement of limbs, plus a quite extraordinary voice. You could call it an acquired taste, or a Marmite-style case of love it or hate it. There are few things I would like to do more now than settle down for a full evening of his singing in some smoky pub; for several reasons, that is not possible. I know others, even among the folk-friendly, who would run a mile at the prospect. The sound he made is perhaps best illustrated by the anagram alter-ego he invented for himself - Elmer P.Bleaty. If there was an old-time singer called Elmer P.Bleaty, he would sound like Peter Bellamy.

The Young Tradition, with him at the helm, made such an extreme row that they almost made The Watersons sound like easy listening. In our house, The Watersons *were* easy listening, because my mum and I had a rare meeting of minds over their eponymous LP. She just loved it; she would play it all day and sing along to tracks like 'Three Score and Ten' whilst she did her interminable house-work. She loved it even more than she loved *The Paul Simon Songbook*, a collection of what were to become Simon and Garfunkel songs, but without the completely unnecessary - to me and my mum - injection of saccharine from Garfunkel. That got the repeat treatment on the Dansette as well. In fact, she wore them out.

Listening to them almost 50 years later, The Watersons retain all the freshness and vitality they brought to the folk scene in the early 60s. Although they were from Hull, the only direct influence you can pick out is from the Copper Family of Sussex. They were sufficiently different, however, to be classified as true originals. Mike and his sisters, Norma and Lal, plus their cousin, John Harrison, had that sibling harmony thing, that runs from the Everlys to the

Unthanks, in trumps. The only thing that grates now is their occasional use on that record of unobtrusive guitar. Unobtrusive it might be, but it still sounds like an intrusion, a chink in the wall of sound. I had the unforgettable experience - well, I say unforgettable, but I can't remember for the life of me where it was - of seeing the original Watersons in their natural environment of a smoky pub room. It remains one of the most exciting sounds I've ever heard and I have the St George's Hotel to thank for it. A BBC documentary called *Travelling for a Living* captured them as they were then, ploughing up and down the country in a knackered old van, singing in folk clubs. Their alternative title for it was 'Grovelling for a Pittance.' The Watersons came up with a highly original reason for splitting up; Norma got a job as a DJ in the West Indies. When they eventually reformed, it was with her husband, Martin Carthy, replacing Harrison.

Lal and Mike are both dead, but their legacy lives on in the current family ensemble - or Royal Family of Folk Music, as they hate to be called - Waterson:Carthy.

There were plenty of instruments played at the St George's, but what I really took away from it was a taste for this previously unfamiliar and exotic business of unaccompanied singing. Ladysmith Black Mambazo hit the same button for me.

That club didn't last very long. The Valley Folk concentrated instead on the club at nearby Bury, a well-established and slightly earnest congregation. I once saw Paul Simon (without Garfunkel) sing an unpaid floor spot there when he was touring British folk clubs trying to get discovered. The general opinion was that he was too lightweight and poppy and probably shouldn't give up his day job.

The loss of the St George's Hotel didn't exactly leave a gap in Bolton. It was boom time for folk clubs. In that one medium-sized town alone, I can remember clubs at pubs like The Cattle Market and The Anchor, some suburban tennis club, a nightclub called The Empress and, most bizarrely, the Central Lancashire Homing Club, the roost of local pigeon fanciers. They can't touch you for it, as someone used to say at least once every night. It was okay, once you got used to the rather odd smells and the occasional feather. These clubs didn't all run at the same time, but they overlapped in such a way that there were always two or three of them on the go. My spiritual home, though, was The Balmoral, an unremarkable pub on Bradshawgate, the main drag for a bad night out. The beer wasn't much good - it still isn't - but it had an upstairs room. And in that room we experienced greatness. There was no microphone, but there was a single free-standing spotlight - which kept on getting nudged and knocked over - so it was a pretty flash operation.

Folk clubs are their own little world, with their own vocabulary. Guests are paid to perform; floor singers are not. Residents run the club and perform.

The residents at The Balmoral were two bearded teachers, Ray and Trev, who took me under their wing, probably because they were amused by someone who looked like an overgrown schoolboy - let's face it, who *was* an overgrown schoolboy - being so enthused by the music. They gave me little jobs to do, like selling the mandatory raffle tickets or re-assembling the spotlight, and let me in for free. Very occasionally, when our residents were guests elsewhere, I would have the task of announcing our guests and floor singers; and, just the once, I sang 'The Rambling Sailor.' When they made their LP, *Tyrants of England* - not on the prestigious Topic label - I wrote the sleeve-notes. They were a mixture of embarrassingly precocious erudition - I must have been 15 or 16 - and ideas filched from Bert Lloyd's *Folk Song in England*. They were also the first thing I ever had published.

Ray Haslam was a lovely bloke and a steady guitarist. Trevor Colluney was more the temperamental virtuoso. On a good night, he could bring the house down - or at least knock the spotlight over - with some dazzling work on the banjo and mandolin. On a bad night, he might never get either tuned to his satisfaction. His roots were in Ireland and it was his playing, as well as Dubliners' LPs, that opened up the musical horizons of that country for me. We also had some rather memorable guests. Two who particularly stick in the mind are Mike Harding and Christy Moore, because in both cases we needed a committee meeting to decide whether to pay them the £5 they wanted. Both went on to earn slightly more than that for a night's work. Christy Moore, believe it or not, was working on building sites and singing in folk clubs for a bit of extra beer money.

Generally speaking, our guests were from the top bracket of local talent rather than national performers: Mike Harding, Harry Boardman, Marie Little, Lea Nicholson and the like. One night we pushed the boat out and booked a group from 'down south' called The Halliard. They turned out to include a young Nic Jones, still tentative as their number two singer, but already playing amazingly. Ray had to be restrained from burning his guitar.

Another night I found that a guest singer called Frank Duffy had lived next door to my mum when they were kids. On the other side must have been the infamous Archibald family, who had so many children that they eventually ran out of names and called the youngest Archibald Archibald. He came back to our house for a cup of tea and a chat with my mum about the old days in New Mills. You don't find Lady GaGa doing that very often.

And who could forget the diminutive Grehan Sisters from County Roscommon? The three of them sang and played a variety of instruments, although I remember the spoons being surprisingly prominent. None of them can have been over 4ft 6; it was like being serenaded by The Krankies. They were a big attraction, though. We had people crammed in everywhere that night. Health and Safety would have had a field day

If you wanted to see bigger artists - in both senses - it could mean a trip to Bury or, more likely, Manchester. That meant travelling on the unfamiliar number 8 bus, which was the wrong colour and took you through places with strange-sounding names, like Irlams o'th'Height. At the end of the line was the Manchester Sports Guild, a little microcosm of alternative music, with jazz on one floor and folk on another. It was there that I first saw the High Level Ranters, A.L. Lloyd, Dominic Behan, Hedy West and plenty of other 'names' on the folk scene. White-jacketed waiters navigated between the tables on three sides of the stage with trays of drinks. It was heady stuff for a teenaged folkie.

Best of all was the night I first heard what many would say is still the best folk club act ever - Martin Carthy and Dave Swarbrick. Both had made their names already; Carthy with The Three City Four and as a solo singer and innovative guitarist, Swarbrick as a startlingly brilliant fiddler with the Ian Campbell Group. Swarb guested on a couple of Carthy LPs before they became a fully-fledged duo with equal billing. Swarbrick was the most charismatic of musicians and played second fiddle to nobody. He was also one of the very few people to read his own obituary, but that is another story. Together, there was nothing to touch them.

The musical chemistry as they pushed each other harder and harder on a set of tunes, or as Swarb accompanied some spell-binding song on fiddle or mandolin, was something to behold. 'Meet you at the end,' they were prone to say as they embarked on another tour-de-force.

Martin Carthy is the closest thing to a super-star that the English folk club scene has produced, but he doesn't act that way. Now over 70, he still does what he has always done, heading off on the train to sing in the upstairs rooms of pubs - because he loves it.

That has not been the whole story, of course. He is a Waterson by marriage, has been a key man in Steeleye Span, Brass Monkey and The Imagined Village. He has played in various combinations with just about anyone who is anyone, sometimes up-front and centre stage, but just as often in support of others. I've seen him play to full concert halls with those three groups, dominate the main stage at major festivals on his own and sing to a handful in a corner of the bar. I was once one of an audience of six at a pub in Standish when something had gone badly wrong with the advertising and he approached it with the same enthusiasm that he would to the Cambridge Folk Festival.

Compared with some other major figures in the folk revival, Carthy has written precious few songs. The ones he has, however, have tended to hit the target. He has also re-made and re-modelled countless songs, sometimes uniting words and music from different sources, sometimes filling in the gaps himself. Some purists might mistrust this process, but he has breathed new life into myriad songs this way.

Martin Carthy is fond of saying that the only harm you can do to the old songs is not to sing them. Mind you, I don't think he has ever heard what I can do to 'The Rambling Sailor,' a song he had included on his own second album.

Perhaps I simply picked the wrong vehicle for my talents. Part of its attraction was that it seemed deceptively easy to sing. In the hands of someone who knew what they were doing, it pretty much sang itself and I suppose I hoped it might do the same for me. Instead, it triggered a vexed internal dialogue that got in the way of singing it at all. Every line, every word almost, seemed fraught with difficulties.

'I am a sailor, brisk and bold.....' No, I'm not, I'm a pupil at the local grammar school. Brisk? Am I singing fast enough? Bold? I think not.

'Long time I've ploughed the ocean...' Just how do you plough an ocean?

Try as I might, I couldn't purvey these sentiments in anything close to a normal accent; it came out as a mixture of Mummerset and Long John Silver. 'I've rambled England and Ireland through, Aaarh Jim lad, for honour and promotion...'

Then there was the issue of my dubious stagecraft. A cupped hand would insist on flying up to an ear, sometimes to both of them. My feet would remain motionless, but the rest of me would writhe like one of those elasticated toy animals, where you press the base and make it do a bad impression of a terrified man singing 'The Rambling Sailor.'

For a while, my singing ambitions went off in a different direction. There was an LP on the prestigious Topic label called *Deep Lancashire* and a few of us fell deeply under its influence. It was claimed at the time to be the biggest seller Topic had ever had, which might not have been saying very much. It was a compilation of songs performed by the likes of Harry Boardman, Mike Harding and the Oldham Tinkers. Lea Nicholson was there as well, with his definitive rendition of 'The Rawtenstall Annual Fair.' It was dangerous stuff, because it made you think: 'I could do that.'

Thus were The Receptacles conceived; or misconceived

would be closer to the mark. Steve and Cliff were two mates from the rugby team. They were both on the small side, so when they packed in on either side they made me look bigger and more awkward than ever, like Long John Baldry (not to be confused with Long John Silver) or Tony Davis of The Spinners. The idea was that we would sing anything off that LP that didn't need accompaniment, because none of us could play an instrument. The trouble was that none of us could sing either. We got away with it as a novelty act at the school disco and that gave us the illusion that we could get away with it in the outside world. We couldn't. I will never forget the baffled faces of the audience at Daisy Hill Cricket Club as we regaled them with stripped down versions of 'The Rawtenstall Annual Fair' and 'A Mon Like Thee' - two embarrassed half-backs and a big, daft bugger in the middle, gyrating as if his clogs were nailed to the stage. Clogs? Certainly. Being a Receptacle was not merely a musical commitment; it was a lifestyle choice. We had some sort of weird, retro young fogey/young folkie thing going on. We had clogs made by a clogger in Leigh. We wore flat caps, mufflers and waistcoats; Steve even had a fob-watch on a silver chain. And this wasn't worn as stage gear or as a joke. It was what we wore on a night out in Westhoughton. How we ever escaped being battered is beyond me.

By this time I had also acquired - or was in the process of acquiring - another fashion accessory. I was allowed to start growing a beard whilst still at school on the flimsy pretext that it went well with my role as a fireman in a play called *The Fire Raisers*. Incredibly, we fire-fighters were also allowed to sit beside the stage when not involved in the action, drinking brown ale and smoking pipes - which I did regularly off-stage by this time. *The Fire Raisers* would have needed to go on a run as long as *The Mousetrap* for me to have shown any dramatic progress in the beard department. In fact, I had a suspicion that someone was coming into my bedroom and shaving it off every night while I slept. We got there in the end, but not in time to give The Receptacles that touch of gravitas that might have saved them.

People have told me since that the problem with The Receptacles was the name. On the contrary, it was the best thing about us. Something else set us apart. Other groups broke up because of artistic differences. We split because of irreconcilable artistic similarities; none of us could play and none of us could sing. Mind you, that hasn't stopped a few people since.

Also on that *Deep Lancashire* record were Dave Brooks and Bernard Wrigley, singers and concertina players from Bolton. Concertinas were huge in Bolton at the time. Bernard's bass concertina was, at any rate; it was the size of a small fridge. For a while, they formed a duo, called - imaginatively - Dave and Bernard, and ran a club at The Anchor on Bury Road. It was a riot, for the simple reason that Bernard was the winner, five years running, of the coveted title of Funniest Man in Bolton. This was well before Peter Kay and all his comedic offspring, but there was hot competition from the rival club at The Cattlemarket across town, run by Bob Williamson. Bob was another who could reduce the upstairs room of a pub to tears of laughter. Plenty of others came through a similar route. The likes of Billy Connolly, Jasper Carrott, Mike Harding, Richard Digance, Tony Capstick and Max Boyce all cut their teeth playing in folk clubs, the jokes and stories gradually taking over from the songs. Like them, Bob Williamson eventually had his own television show. Bernard never quite achieved that, nor did he have a chart single like Harding's 'Rochdale Cowboy,' although his version of 'Nellie the Elephant' must have come close. For my money, though, he was funnier than any of them. Give him a room up a flight of stairs, a locked door and no other means of escape and he could reduce any audience to rubble. I was, briefly, his unofficial roadie; surely the most useless roadie of all time, as I couldn't drive. I was, however, twice as useful as the one-armed Dave Brady when it came to heaving bass concertinas around.

For four or five nights, Bernard delivered basically the same show to a different folk club somewhere in the north of England. It wasn't merely as funny when you heard it for the fifth time, it was funnier. That is what you call a rare gift.

He made two nominally serious albums for the prestigious Topic label, although both had their hilarious moments. He is a versatile actor, who has been on *Coronation Street* almost as often as Ken Barlow. But he was most spectacularly in his element presiding over the club at The Anchor - the Anchor-Chief, as he liked to be known, which gives you some idea of the sophistication of the humour. It created such a knock-about atmosphere that I thought I might have another bash at 'The Rambling Sailor.' If I couldn't get away with it there, I couldn't get away with it anywhere.

On reflection, I decided that my version of this fine, old song was somewhat unfocussed. A bit too rambling, to be honest, and the shadow of Rambling Syd Rumpo from *Round the Horne* hung over it like a bad smell. What I needed to do, I decided, was to study the damned thing in detail. I listened to proper singers' versions; Carthy, Lloyd, Dave Burland, Tony Rose. I read up about it. I investigated related songs. What I discovered was that it probably came from the 1820s and was predated by a song called 'The Rambling Soldier' - still no Rambling Sixth-Former, unfortunately. Both songs were printed regularly on broadsides - commercial song-sheets - through the 19th century, but it was the Sailor variant that entered the oral tradition; that is to say, it was the one people liked to sing. Ralph Vaughan Williams, no less, collected it from a singer called Peter Verral in Horsham, Sussex in 1907. There is also a related song called 'The Trim-Rigged Doxy,' with the same basic story but the opposite moral. Armed with this information, I inevitably became even more confused. There was now the option of starting not with 'I am a sailor.....' but with 'I am a soldier, blithe and gay.....' I think not. Having made the policy decision to stick with the naval theme, we have the classic case-study of a sailor with a girl in every port.

> 'And if you want to know my name, my name it is Young Johnson ..... I've got a commission from the King to court all girls [as] is handsome.'

In his sleeve notes to the first Spiers and Boden album, *Through and Through,* Jon Boden calls this 'one of the lesser-known royal appointments,' but Young Johnson seems to have carried out his duties with gusto. The song is effectively an account of a couple of conquests, followed by a promise of more of the same.

> 'And then I rose up with the dawn
> Just as the day was peeping.
> On tiptoe down the stairs I went
> And I left my love a-sleeping.
> And if she waits until I come
> She may lie there till the day of her doom;
> I'll court some other girl in their room
> And I'll be the rambling sailor.'

That's what you might call the happy ending, but Carthy's 'Rambling Sailor' and the mariner in anything called 'The

Trim-Rigged Doxy' finish on a less triumphal note: 'I think her little fire-bucket burnt my bob-stay through ..... That saucy little trim-rigged doxy.'

Imagine trying to sing that without moving your feet. I'm still a little vague about what a bob-stay does, but the fire-bucket I instinctively understood. And, just for good measure, she robs him as well. That's how user-friendly folk song can be. Centuries before interactive TV gave viewers a choice of ending, the Folk were offering the same facility. You can choose in the case, for instance, whether your sailor gets a dose of the clap, or merely a round of applause.

I doubt whether anything ever sung at The Anchor had been more intensively researched, but it still didn't sound right - not even to me, let alone the audience. Perhaps it was the tune, rather than the words, that was the trouble. It seemed straightforward enough, but it's in the notoriously tricky mixolydian mode and littered with bear-traps for the unwary. I won't even try to explain what the mixolydian mode is, except to say that, if you are intent on singing out of tune, it is the logical place to start. Bernard tells me that there is a tape of this performance somewhere. That is where it should stay - somewhere unspecified and unreachable.

The conventional wisdom during the folk revival of the Sixties and Seventies was that, if you wanted to know how to do it, you had to listen to the source singers - elderly chaps (for the most part) who had kept the old songs alive. You didn't have to sit and wait for them to come to you; you could go to them. In the absence of Mr Verral of Horsham, the best place to start was Rottingdean. Whilst Vaughan Williams was noting down the words and music of 'The Rambling Sailor,' there was a treasury of traditional song a few miles away that he never discovered. The Copper Family of Rottingdean are generations of singers who have preserved a repertoire of rural song unmatched anywhere in the country. Their singing style is instantly recognisable, their influence on revival performers impossible to overstate and, if you timed it right, you could have your pint pulled by one or other of them.

The Coppers at the time were Bob and his cousin, Ron. Although they both sang solo occasionally, their real forte was two-part harmony as passed down to them by their respective fathers, Jim and John. As a very rough guide, Bob sang the melody line and Ron the bass. It's a soundtrack for an idyllic England, with sheep grazing on the cliff-tops. My girlfriend at the time had a bit of interest in this sort of thing, or at least decided to humour me, so she was easy to talk into a weekend away 'near Brighton.' Thus it was that we were in the public bar of the Queen Victoria in Rottingdean, where, on the other side of the Harvey's Bitter pumps was Ron Copper. I had to tell him, as thousands of others must, how much I had enjoyed his family's songs. 'Have you got a favourite?' Ron asked. I had to admit to a particular liking for 'Spencer the Rover,' an innocuous little tale of a man with a mid-life crisis who leaves home and goes walkabout, then has a change of heart and goes back. It's not *War and Peace*, but it is set to a majestic tune and has been a magnet for all manner of singers since Ron and Bob dusted it off. The version many people will have stumbled upon is the one by John Martyn, the cult hero singer and guitarist. The one that will stay with me, though, is the one sung by Ron Copper in the vault of the Queen Victoria, before it got busy that Friday evening.

> 'These words were composed by Spencer the Rover ..... Who travelled Great Britain and most parts of Wales....' [Folk's grasp of geography could be a little tenuous.]

He even threw in a couple of other songs before the locals, who had no doubt seen all this before, started rolling their eyes, holding up their empty glasses and drumming their fingers on the bar. The trip was already a roaring success as far as I was concerned, although Sara was later heard to complain that it had been less a romantic weekend in Brighton than a rotten weekend in Rottingdean.

That was not the last time I mithered some aging icon of English folk-song. I had already seen Fred Jordan sing at various festivals, including Keele, and his album, *Songs of a Shropshire Farm Worker*, was a bit of a cult classic. In his mole-skin breeches and lop-sided cap, he was as big a celebrity as a Shropshire farm worker could be. A lot of the traditional singers 'discovered' by the folk revival - even the great ones like Harry Cox and Sam Larner - were old men, with old men's voices. Their phrasing and delivery could still be an education, but the actual singing voice could be something of a challenge. Fred Jordan, on the other hand, was very much in his prime and in full voice when he became known to the world beyond Salop. When I found myself living in that county, therefore, it was only a matter of time before I got on my motorbike and went to Aston Munslow to pay my respects. I seem to remember that I had to send him a postcard to confirm the arrangements. It was a blazing hot day - it always was during the three summers when I worked in Shropshire - and Fred was working on his smallholding next to his cottage. By way of refreshment, he had a stone jar of cold tea and he was in the same gear he wore when he was singing in a pub or at a festival. He was like something from a different century - and I don't mean the 21st. After a bit of discussion about runner beans and the like, we repaired to the cottage and drank some cold tea. There, much to the bemusement of the photographer from the *South Shropshire Journal,* who had arrived by this time, he sang a few songs and talked about his life. He had a particularly fine version of 'The Outlandish Knight,' which he had learnt in his youth from local gypsies in Corve Dale and called 'Six Pretty Maids.' It was an early reminder for me of the role of the often-hated Roma and travelling populations in keeping songs alive. Almost forty years later, two of the singers I've seen most recently - June Tabor and Sam Lee - have made the same point.

Fred also had a grand version of 'John Barleycorn,' but his signature tune was probably 'The Farmer's Boy,' a singalong pub favourite. It's one of those annoying songs you are liable to have heard without realising it: 'To plough and sow and reap and mow and be a farmer's boy ..... And be a farmer's boy.....'

There was nothing of the rural bumpkin about him, however; he was a long way from being the typical horny-handed son of the soil. He might have spent most of his life as a farm labourer, but that was largely by choice. At school in Ludlow, he was top of the class and destined for further studies, but left at 14 to work on a farm in Corve Dale, despite teachers and family trying to persuade him to stay on. His reason was simply that farm-work, especially with horses, was the life he wanted; working in the open air by day, singing in pubs in Ludlow and Corve Dale by night. The BBC first stuck a microphone in front of him in 1952 when he was 30 and that life was never quite the same again. He was taken up by the folk revival as a rare example of a genuine traditional singer with his voice intact. That voice was a clear, ringing tenor, with heavy use of vibrato. It took him from village pubs like The Sun in Corfton and The Tally Ho in Bouldon to The Festival Hall and The Royal Albert Hall. It also made him as close to a celebrity as you could be in the back-water of a back-water that was Corve Dale. I was a long way from being the first to make the pilgrimage to visit him in Aston Munslow. In fact, I was following in some distinguished tyre-tracks. In 1967, no less a literary figure than Angela Carter had descended on the Corve to interview him for *New Society*.

She reported on his living arrangements: 'Fred Jordan's home is stoutly built and freshly creosoted. It is a sensible arrangement for a country bachelor to live in such a shed for it is, in effect, a detached bed-sitting room.'

I think he had done a bit more spring cleaning for *New Society* than he did for the *South Shropshire Journal* and the distinguished novelist was equally impressed with his singing. 'His style is straightforward, sweet and dignified. He always looks very grave and intent when he sings, as if it were a very serious affair. In the manner of the true traditional singer, he inclines to let his personality retire behind the song, with neither physical gesture nor change of face.'

Ms Carter clearly got her article; so did I, although I think that a three-part series was more than they were expecting at the *South Shropshire Journal*. He was well used to being interviewed by this stage. In fact, there is an 'Angela' thread developing here, because on one of his furthest-flung singing bookings in Plymouth he had been interrogated by a junior reporter named Angela Rippon. There was just one disappointment for me. 'The Rambling Sailor?' said Fred Jordan. 'No, I never heard that one.'

I probably came off my motorbike on my way back to my freshly creosoted country bachelor's shed in a village near Oakengates. I usually did after this sort of expedition. A useful tip for you: Never attempt to ride a motorbike in clogs.

On another foray, I fixed my throttle cable - a horribly vulnerable area on a CZ 125 - with the help of the chap I'd just interviewed, a Colonel Faithfull. Marianne's uncle, I believe, but I was warned before I went to visit him at his owl sanctuary not to mention *Girl on a Motorcycle*, Mars bars or Mick Jagger.

A few miles from Fred Jordan, in Aston on Clun, lived the Kirkpatricks; John K was and is the king of squeezebox players - accordion, melodeon and Anglo concertina (not to be confused with the English concertina.) He has squeezed his boxes with just about everyone, written a great heap of songs and tunes, played a stint with Steeleye Span and occupies a central role with the mightily influential Brass Monkey. His wife, Sue Harris, was, if not the world's number one hammered dulcimer player, then undeniably the best in Shropshire. And the little, sandy-haired toddler, showing far too much interest in my motorbike, must have been Benji Kirkpatrick, now the master of all things stringed in Bellowhead. Is there anybody in folk music, you are entitled to ask, who is not connected, directly or indirectly, with everyone else? Given a big enough sheet of graph paper and plenty of colour-coded felt-tips, I believe I could answer that question.

In my book, John Kirkpatrick was one of the folk heroes of the 1970s and thereafter. I've already mentioned a few of the others; Martin Carthy and Dave Swarbrick, Nic Jones, Tony Rose, Dick Gaughan, Robin and Barry Dransfield. It was a golden era, but you will have to take my word for that to some extent, because a lot of the best albums of the time are kept under lock and key by a rights-owner who refuses to release them on CD.

You will also have to believe me, or his various other devotees, on the subject of what a great performer Peter

Bellamy was, because he killed himself in 1991. That was a tragically premature end to a life that makes you ask 'How the hell did he cram all that in?' Quite apart from founding The Young Tradition and singing solo in the upstairs rooms of a million pubs, he was responsible for two monumental bodies of work: *The Transports*, a ballad-opera on an epic scale; and the setting to music of scores and scores of Rudyard Kipling's poems. It is hard to imagine a more Quixotic, unfashionable task to take on than turning the work of the great poet of the British Raj unto folk-club fodder. Was it even possible as a leftie to listen to it without a shudder of rejection? Somehow, possibly because he wrote such exceedingly good tunes, he made it work. But not to his own satisfaction, obviously. One final battle honour; he was the man who regaled the staunchly traditional - 'purist' even (definition to follow) - club in Nottingham with a Chuck Berry song. History does not record which Chuck Berry song; hopefully not 'My Ding-a-Ling.'

The economics of folk clubs were always a nightmare. Packing enough people into a room to pay enough on the door to make it worthwhile for one or more performers to travel long distances to sing a few songs or play a few tunes; the numbers never really added up. One thing for sure - nobody ever got rich that way. The days when towns had several folk clubs have gone; most of what you might call small-scale music takes place in arts centres and the like - places like The Met in Bury, The Mechanics in Burnley and the Hebden Bridge Trades Club. That is where much of the scene has migrated. There are exceptions; the Bothy Folk Club in Southport is coming up for its 50th anniversary. Apart from booking young, up-and-coming musicians, it is also hooked into what, if it was golf or tennis, would be termed a veterans' tour - performers who were big in the 70s and 80s and still know how to work a folk club audience now. I've seen the likes of Vin Garbutt, Chris Foster and Archie Fisher there, but the singer who really summed it all up for me was Dave Burland. He might look like a bouncer at a particularly rough Yorkshire nightclub, but he has a voice as warm and mellow as rhubarb crumble. He was huge in the 80s and he's not exactly small now. He has the knack of stripping something like the Boomtown Rats' 'I Don't Like Mondays' of its pop-star posturing to reveal the good song beneath. At Southport, he chuckled as he told us about his grandson, who had found him packing his guitar that afternoon.

'Have you got "a gig", granddad?' - words he probably never thought he would hear when he was a young buck in the folk clubs.

Still, at least he remembered his guitar. One of the residents - remember them? The unpaid cannon fodder - opened up his case on stage recently and found....nothing. In a senior moment, he had left his instrument at home, leaving him with the alternatives of playing air guitar or apologising and coming back the following week. The audience was sympathetic and understanding; like him, we are not getting any younger.

There are still similar folk clubs scattered around the United Kingdom, but if I were to send you to a place that really keeps the old flame glimmering, you would have to make a rather longer trip. Devonport is a pleasant, self-contained little suburb, a 20 minute ferry-ride across the harbour from Auckland. Like much in New Zealand, it is a heady mix of the cosily familiar and the frankly bizarre. Walk up the main street and you come to a volcano; dormant, to the best of my knowledge, and one of the many that make up the local landscape. Follow the winding road up the volcano and you come to a sort of bunker - the remains of a Second

World War gun emplacement. Go inside on the right night of the week and you're in the warm glow of an idealised 1960s British folk club. An open fire, a few six-packs of Lion Red from the bottle-shop down the hill and complimentary cheese and biscuits at half-time. You probably don't even have to slog up the volcano; someone in a battered ute will pull in and give you a lift. The first time I went to Devonport Folk Club, a young Kiwi lad was singing songs from the first Young Tradition LP; the last time, an Irishman was singing his own songs about the pearl fisheries of Broome in Western Australia. It might be 13,000 miles from the Balmoral or the Bothy, but I've rarely felt so much at home.

Ewan MacColl and the Folk Police

NO less an authority than Ewan MacColl, in his autobiography *Journeyman*, made the point that the only thing folk clubs had in common was smoke. He should know. At the end of 1968, he calculated that he and Peggy Seeger - his wife, accompanist and muse - had sung at 482 of them.

Even that was only skimming the surface; his estimate is that, at the high-water mark of the folk revival, there were 2,500 in the country, every one of them emitting its cloud of fug. If Roy Castle was the best-known victim of passive smoking in the variety and workingmen's clubs, then the Smoke of the Folk - there's a song there somewhere - often spiced-up with extra ingredients, must have claimed a few lungs as well. Flash guitarists used to have a technique on impaling a fag on the end of a string to keep it burning until the end of the next number. Warning: Do not attempt this with a nylon-strung guitar.

Folk clubs did come in all shapes, sizes and styles.

They ranged in attitude from knock-about piss-ups to the deeply serious and evangelical. MacColl was at the latter end of that spectrum. His club in London, Ballads and Blues, later the Singers' Club, was famous - even infamous - for its policy of only allowing performers to sing material from their own native tradition. This was a reaction to the American domination left over from the skiffle boom and could be justified as a piece of positive discrimination aimed at keeping British music alive. On the other hand, it could be resented as proscriptive and Stalinist. There was a time when he might have taken that as a compliment. One of his early songs was a paean of praise to Uncle Joe, mercifully dropped from his later repertoire.

MacColl, the founding father of the folk revival, was inspiring and intimidating in equal measure. Inspiring because of the range of his song-writing, which at its best yielded work which seems likely to be indestructible, and the sheer power and poise of his singing. Intimidating because he always knew for a fact that his way was the right way and had little but withering scorn for those who wanted to go in a different direction, politically or musically.

The question of his own identity was not a simple one. He was born in 1915, not in Scotland, as he sometimes allowed others to think, but in the dowie dens of Salford; not as Ewan MacColl, but plain Jimmie Miller. It begs the mischievous question of whether, by his own rules, he was really allowed to sing Scot songs. MacColl was a stage name adopted later, when he was principally an actor, but he was still Jimmie Miller when he caught the train to Hayfield and his first intersection with our family history.

It was 1932 and he was 17-years-old and already politically active. That was how he came to be involved in the Mass Trespass on Kinder Scout.

The fight for public access to the moors of the Peak District had been simmering for some time, but this was its big set-piece.

My dad, Stanley Levi Hadfield, was nine months younger and already the sole bread-winner for his widowed mother. He remembers the impact on the village of the demonstrators' arrival. 'As far as we were concerned, they were just a load of trouble-makers from Salford,' he tells me. Some of his contemporaries were hired as extra help for the game-keepers that day, but not him; nor, he thinks, Arthur Lowe - later Capt Mainwaring in *Dad's Army* - with whom he had been at school in Hayfield. Still, there were no doubts where his sympathies lay. Right time, right place, wrong side; two out of three isn't bad. There's a rather splendid irony, though, in that few people were destined to benefit more than he from open access to the moors. In later life, he walked all the famous long-distance routes - the Coast to Coast, Offa's Dyke and, of course, the Pennine Way, which crosses the once forbidden moors of Kinder. Thank you, Salford trouble-makers, he now has the good grace to say.

Kinder Scout is one of those northern English hills whose summit is a decided let-down. It's old rock, ground down to a boggy plateau, rather than sharpened to a peak. The approaches to it, however, are magnificent and my dad and I have always been drawn back to it. The little quarry where the trespassers gathered is now a car-park. We're too tight to pay-and-display, so we park on the road. The next time we do it, he will be pushing 99, so he has had his money's worth out of the Mass Trespassers of 1932.

Ewan MacColl was always drawn back to the same hills. He particularly liked to stay at the pub in Little Hayfield, because that was where another Salford radical, Friedrich Engels, spent weekends with his bit-on-the-side.

My dad wouldn't know about that. 'We never had much call to go to Little Hayfield,' he tells me. It's about a mile away and this is a man who, in his sixties, walked from St Bees to Robin Hood's Bay.

Contrary to popular belief, Ewan MacColl did not write 'The Manchester Rambler' to be sung on the Kinder Trespass, but a couple of years later, to commemorate it. It's one of those songs that, even if you think you've never heard it, you almost certainly have done - it or a variant.

> 'I'm a rambler, I'm a rambler from Manchester way.
> 'I get all my pleasure the hard moorland way.
> 'I may be a wage-slave on Monday,
> 'But I am a free man on Sunday.'

Actually, as a sports-writer, I've far more often been a wage-slave on Sunday and a free man on Monday (subject to evening fixtures) but the idea holds good. Besides, the 'Rambler' has proved to be the most malleable of songs. A few years after it was written, MacColl heard it sung and described as a traditional song from British Columbia.

'I'm a logger, I'm a logger, from up BC way.....' Almost any job, hobby or affiliation will fit the template, so it has cropped up in too many different guises to number. It was a long way from being Ewan MacColl's first song - he had been churning out political songs since his early teens. It was, however, the first one to become famous and the first of four, from all the hundreds he wrote, which illuminate, if not his whole career, then a significant slice of it.

The second is another song that you can hardly have avoided without blocking your ears with sealing wax - 'Dirty Old Town.' Like a few of MacColl's greatest hits, it was written almost by accident, in this case to cover for a scene change in a play called *Landscape With Chimneys*, which he wrote in 1950 for Joan Littlewood's Theatre Workshop. It was a little throwaway that has developed an unstoppable life of its own.

The first version I heard must have been on an Ian Campbell Group LP, which helpfully included the hint in the sleeve notes that there was a danger of it sounding like the theme music to a B-feature Western ..... and then served it up sounding exactly like the theme music to a B-feature Western. Much more familiar now would be The Pogues' somehow appropriately rough and ready version. The setting in which it really proves how deeply it has been absorbed, however, is on the terraces of Salford's rugby league club. Okay, the words get a bit garbled; did you meet your love 'on the gasworks croft' or 'by the gasworks cross,' before you 'dreamed a dream by the old canal'?

It's never been quite what the Salford tourist department had in mind, but it sums up one English city - town is a bit of a slight - better than any other song.

Later in the Fifties, MacColl embarked on one of the great achievements of his life - the *Radio Ballads*. There had been nothing on the BBC remotely like the blend of song, music and the words of ordinary people that he put together. Many of us would say there has been nothing to better it since.

The first of the series was *The Ballad of John Axon*, about a train driver who, like Casey Jones, lost his life but saved his passengers when his brakes failed on the run between Stockport and Dove Holes in Derbyshire.

He made memorable musical documentaries on subjects as diverse as coal-mining, gypsies and boxing. The one which has always stuck in my mind, though, is *Singing the Fishing*, possibly because I listened to it in the early Sixties, on the big steam wireless in my grandma's flat in New Mills, where she was probably the only person in Britain who warmed-up packets of Smith's crisps in the oven by the fireplace. Now that was luxury; so was listening to Ewan MacColl singing 'Shoals of Herring,' intercut with the voices of East Coast fishermen describing the life. All the *Radio Ballads* were good; *Singing the Fishing* was, to my mind, just about perfect. As for 'Shoals,' it was absorbed into the tradition as effortlessly as 'the silver darlings' gliding with the tide. People who have never heard of Ewan MacColl or the *Radio Ballads* sing it and assume that it has always been there.

Much the same applies to another unforgettable MacColl song, 'The First Time Ever I Saw Your Face,' the story of which is more of an unlikely journey than any fishing voyage in the North Sea.

The romantic legend is that Ewan wrote it for Peggy and sang it down the phone to her in America. He was supposed to be there on tour as well, but had been refused entry because of his Communist sympathies, which was a bit like barring the Pope for his Catholic tendencies. MacColl was a card-carrying member of the Communist Party of Great Britain - the one that considered all the Monty Pythonesqe array of other Communist parties a bit flippant. Peggy was an equally convinced Communist, but she was their commie and her husband was ours. She could get into America, but he couldn't; she toured on her own and Ewan came up with a new song for her to sing.

Here's a strange thing, though; although it was 'her' song, I distinctly remember him singing it - and it being sublime. To be honest, I was never that wild about Peggy's version, although that was the one that spread hither and thither and was picked up by other singers after she performed it for the first time in a concert in Los Angeles. The Kingston Trio released a bowdlerised version, which - pathetically - replaced 'The first time ever I lay with you' with 'The first time ever I danced with you.' Peter, Paul and Mary recorded it, as did everyone up to and including Elvis Presley. Exciting times for the author, then? Not really; MacColl says in *Journeyman* that: 'It made singularly little impression on me. I was scarcely conscious of it. I had lots of other things on my mind, not least of which was the need to earn a living.'

So the royalties must have been welcome? MacColl describes them as '...a pittance and not enough for luxuries like food. It wasn't until 1971 when Roberta Flack recorded her soul version of the song that I became aware of having written a commercially successful 'hit'. At first I didn't realise how successful ..... I was unimpressed and continued to be unimpressed.'

He was, of course, unlikely to start turning cartwheels over the way that the wicked old market-place had effectively provided him with a pension. The closest he gets to celebrating its Grammy-winning fame is to describe it as... 'a kind of watershed in our lives. Both Peggy and I were now in a position to spend a lot more time on political songwriting.' It might have been the great romantic gesture of their lives, but its importance was in its relevance to the struggle.

Not everybody was having any of this Ewan and Peggy legend. To some, they were little more than charlatans. The star witness for the prosecution has to be Shirley Collins, a remarkable singer herself, almost a neighbour of the Copper Family in Sussex and one-time wife of Ashley Hutchings, a founder of both Fairport Convention and Steeleye Span. (Where's that Folk Family Tree when you need it?)

In an interview by Jo Breeze in the magazine *FRoots* in 2012, she recalls one incident early in her singing career and broadens it out to explain her fierce antipathy to the couple.

> 'When I was very young and naïve, first in London and crazy about anything to do with folk music at all, I had gone to hear Ewan MacColl sing. He invited me to go back to his house to see his big collection of folk song books. Of course, what I hadn't realised was that he was asking me to go and 'see his etchings' ..... as soon as I stepped inside he started taking his shirt off and he had the most awful toad-like speckled skin - and I just fled!'

She had no bus-fare and never did get to browse his library.

> 'Besides, I quickly moved away from wanting to have anything to do with that lot, so pompous and so pretentious. And they were quite malicious as well; they were not kind people. Cold people. Brisk and cold.
>
> 'This great love affair between him and Peggy; they obviously were in love, but I thought "how could anybody fall in love with Ewan?" I'm not fond of either of them, but they weren't fond of me.
>
> 'I thought what they were doing was not right, the way they were teaching singing and making rules. I didn't think they were very good singers themselves and certainly not good traditional singers.

> '.....Like Ewan, when he started singing he would turn a chair around, sit astride it, face the audience, stick his hand behind his ear - it was just pretentious and had nothing to do with the songs. It had all to do with promoting this image, which drove me absolutely nuts.'

Ewan MacColl, were he still alive, could hardly complain if others had strong opinions about him, pro and anti, because he was a man of strong and outspoken opinions himself. He was not one to mince his words on the subject of writers and singers whose work he considered inferior, especially inferior to the traditional material which, alongside his own songs, formed the other half of his repertoire. He had a special contempt for Bob Dylan, which comes through loud and clear in a piece he contributed to *Sing Out* magazine in 1965.

> 'Our traditional songs and ballads are the creation of extraordinary artists working inside ..... rules made over time. But what of Bobby [sic] Dylan? scream the outraged teenagers. Only a non-critical audience, nourished on the watery pap of pop music could have fallen for such tenth-rate drivel.'

There is a photograph of Dylan making one of his first appearances in a London folk club. Glowering in the background is the unmistakeable figure of MacColl. It is safe to say that he does not appear to be enjoying the performance. In fact, he looks like a man in severe pain from his piles. It's not so much the old gunslinger/young gunslinger thing; more of a fundamental disagreement about what the gun is for. To MacColl, the singer and the song were always at the service of the politics; Dylan couldn't wait to dump that burden.

And yet it was possible to be enthusiastic about both, and as excited by the prospect of Ewan MacColl at Bolton Folk Club as by Bob Dylan at the Free Trade Hall.

Booking Ewan and Peggy was not like booking any other guests. You got a list of their requirements, which you had to agree to provide. If they had been a rock band, this would have been known as 'the rider' and would have specified particular colours of Smarties and preferred cuvées and vintages of Champagne. In this case, it demanded a high-backed chair, no bar in the room and definitely no cash register. The old toad-impersonator straddled the chair in the approved manner - the same pose adopted by Christine Keeler in a famous nude photo, except that Ewan, mercifully, kept his gear on - and sang like an angel. Some of his recordings from this time now sound rather mannered. I can only say that, live and in the flesh, as it were, there was magic in the way he used those old tonsils to hold the upstairs room of the Balmoral in thrall. There were people everywhere that night; perched on the window-sills, shoved under tables, hanging from chandeliers. We had made it all-ticket and sold out weeks in advance, but there was still a queue of punters on the stairs, hoping that they might sneak in on the blind-side. The maestro was in fine voice and sang plenty of everyone's favourites, a couple of 20-verse Scots ballads during which you could hear a pin drop, a sprinkling of north-west industrial songs, including, I'm pretty sure, 'The Four-Loom Weaver,' and a couple of what used to be called protest songs about Vietnam. Peggy sang 'The First Time Ever.....' and it was undeniably spell-binding. Her accompaniments on guitar and, especially, banjo leapt off the six-inch high stage as they never did on record.

I don't know whether it was part of the contract, but it was understood that they got a feed at the end of the night, preferably at the best Indian restaurant in town. In Bolton in the mid-Sixties, there was only one - The Kismet at the top of Bank Street. I don't know either whether it was expected that the club organisers went along too, but we did; Trev and his girlfriend, Barbara, Ray and his wife, Anne ..... and me. I must have done particularly sterling work with the spotlight and the raffle tickets that week, because this felt like a great honour - and still does. It was daunting, though, to find myself sitting next to the great man and expected to hold my own in erudite conversation with him for the next couple of hours. I was 15 or 16; I should have been listening to the Monkees or the Dave Clark Five. Instead, I was on the receiving end of a two-hour tutorial on British folk song from a god come down from Olympus. He talked, I listened. He told me how I'd come to folk music and why I loved it the way I did. I picked my way through the poppadoms and the chicken vindaloo that someone told me was a good, mild curry to start on. I'd never had a proper curry before, although my mum did something exotic and mysterious with sultanas at home.

I'd also never drunk a full bottle of wine. Can it really have been Mateus Rosé? Yes, I do believe it was; the rest of the evening is slightly hazy. One thing I do remember, though, is Ewan MacColl putting me on the spot and testing my knowledge of a particular Scots border ballad.

'Of course, you know the ballad of "Lamkin",' he said confidently. I didn't. I somehow had it mixed up with 'Tamlin,' so he was obliged to jog my memory - and that of the bemused Indian waiters - by singing a couple of verses. He had plenty to choose from, because 'Lamkin' - better known in an English version called 'Long Lankin' - is one of those ballads that can be as long as you want it to be. If you feel you're running short, you can always drag a few extra verses in from elsewhere.

It is also one of the cruellest, bloodiest ballads in the canon, the sort of thing that could have inspired Charlie Manson and his gang. In essence, the story is this: Lord has work done on castle, but neglects to pay the mason, one Lamkin or Lankin; whilst Lord is away somewhere, the False Nurse, who has some unspecified grievance of her own, lets him in; the two of them take the baby - often, but not always, named Johnson - and 'prick him all over with a pin'; that wakes the Lady, who is persuaded to come down and comfort him and is duly killed by Lamkin; the Lord comes home, finds out what has happened, hangs Lamkin and burns the False Nurse at the stake. Just an ordinary, everyday story of border folk.

For all the range and scope of his work, it was the big ballads that MacColl regarded as the pinnacle of folk song. Once you got him going on 'Lamkin,' there was no stopping him.

He was re-thinking his whole approach to singing such songs at the time. Employing the theatrical techniques of Stanislavski, he tried to get inside the characters. What, for instance, is the motivation of the False Nurse? What is the likely social background of the murderous Lamkin? His reaction seems a little extreme for a workman whose bill hasn't been paid. More wine, more vindaloo.

If I seem to remember this part of the conversation suspiciously well, there is a reason for that. In *Journeyman,* MacColl gives a detailed description of how he tackles 'Lamkin' in particular and the big ballads in general. As I read it, I thought: 'Hang on. I've heard this before.' It was pretty much the seminar that he gave me in The Kismet more than

20 years earlier. I could claim that he was trying out his theories on me. After the wine and the curry, I was not merely a captive audience, but a chloroformed patient on the operating table. Naturally, I was out of my depth, but at least he kept his shirt on.

I went back to have a look at Bank Street recently. The Kismet restaurant is long gone, but there are a few other personal landmarks around. There's the club where I saw The Who, there's the pub where my son's mates' band plays and where my middle daughter lost her passport the night before she was due to fly to Australia. There's Bank Street Taxis, where a cab ran over my foot at the end of a particularly good night out and I never even noticed. There's the Unitarian Chapel, where I married Ruth. They should really have a big flashing neon sign on the roof: 'We marry anyone.' The Unitarians have pretty much cornered the market in awkward alliances - a neutral venue for odd combinations like a guilty lapsed Catholic and an atheistic Primitive Methodist. Ruth came down the aisle to De Dannan's version of 'The Entry of the Queen of Sheba' and we were all then harangued for half an hour by the Rev Austin Fitzpatrick. His text - how wronged he had been by the local press and what an irony it was that he should be officiating at the wedding of one of the bastards. The whole occasion went with a swing after that.

Sometimes, it seems to me that Bolton is just the place where I happen to have lived for a big slice of my life and that I have no real roots there. Then I walk down Bank Street - not a very long street - and think that I have inadvertently left a few footprints around the place - and not just at the taxi rank. The top end of it, though, will always be synonymous to me with Ewan MacColl and the massive influence his personality exerted on the folk scene. It was not just 'The First

Time Ever I Saw Your Face' that night; it was also The First Time Ever I Ate a Curry and The First Time Ever I Drank a Bottle of Wine. How I avoided making it The First Time Ever I Spewed in the Gutter is a minor miracle.

I can't really claim to have had singing lessons from Ewan MacColl, or perhaps, in a round-about, indirect sort of way, I can. One of the many aspects of his work which people tended to find sinister was The Critics Group. Perhaps, like The Receptacles, the first problem was with the name. All that it denoted, MacColl insists in his autobiography, was a critical approach to their own singing. The idea was that a number of singers should get together and their efforts should be analysed and criticised by each other, or, if you were very lucky, by the Big Man himself. As terrifying concepts go, that rates pretty high.

The impression that the rest of the inhabitants of Planet Folk had was that it was them being criticised by this rarified elite who were the only ones who knew how it should be done. They were the Folk Police's Flying Squad. As far as MacColl's own (ahem) critics were concerned, they might as well have called themselves the Stasi.

Like a clandestine political movement, they spread the word through underground cells. Just by accident, I stumbled into one. The Critics had a particularly active branch in Stoke-on-Trent, which included people of the calibre of Phil Colclough, who wrote perhaps the definitive song about The Troubles, 'Song for Ireland,' which was recorded by, among others, Dick Gaughan. The spin-off from that was a sub-branch on the campus at Keele University, where I was in the early stages of getting to grips with student life. Somewhere along the line I met Jeff Lowe, a singer, concertina-player, revolutionary Marxist and sometime member of the Critics Group, who invited me to the weekly 'analyse and criticise' sessions in his post-graduate flat. The objective was that each of us should work on a particular song, eventually exposing a 'finished' version to the scrutiny of our peers.

But it's one thing for Phil Colclough to sing 'Song for Ireland' or some other marvellous thing he'd written, and quite another for me to resume hostilities with 'The Rambling Sailor.' It had to be done, but it was not made easier by the knowledge that some of my mates, including, I regret to say, a lapsed Receptacle, were outside the window, sniggering.

We had a few weeks of general work-shopping; listening to records of traditional singers, debating the merits of different versions, that sort of thing. All the time, though, the day was getting closer when I would have to stand up in front of some proper singers and give them 'The Rambling Sailor,' unexpurgated and unaccompanied.

I had bought into the fundamental precepts of MacColl/Critics-style singing. They start with an assertion that there is no physiological difference between a singer and a non-singer. In other words, it is all nurture and no nature. The technical key to it all is to sing with the throat, rather than the chest - which is what opera-singers use and look what a horrible noise they make. The other rule I remember was that there should by no dynamic variation within a song; no louder or quieter bits. I thought I could manage the tension in the throat part; I had tension from the soles of my clogs to the top of my head.

When my turn came, I tried not to sway around, nor to fluctuate in volume or - a real trap, this one - speed. I kept the decoration to a minimum and strove to eliminate the Long John Silver accent I was prone to slip into. In other words, I gave it my best shot.

When I finished, there was silence in the bed-sit. Jeff

Lowe was not, by nature, an unkind person. 'You know what?' he said eventually. 'That almost worked - the way you sort of talked it.'

Well, there was a lot I could have said to that. 'I'll have you know,' I might have said, 'that there is a long and honourable tradition of the talking blues as a vehicle for radical critiques of society.' I could have pointed him towards two blokes in North America - Tom Waits and Leonard Cohen - who were destined to pretty much abandon singing their songs in favour of speaking them - and would make a fortune in the process. I could, if I had the slightest inkling about it, have claimed to be introducing them to Rap, before anyone thought of calling it that.

In the end, I didn't say any of that. I just said 'Thank you,' the way people say it to Alan Sugar or Simon Cowell. I was basking in the glow of the best review I ever had or hoped to have. 'It almost worked' - I'll have that on my first LP or on my tombstone, whichever comes first.

I met Jeff Lowe again a couple of years later. He had got a particularly bad dose of religion and had renounced all his political activism. The Kalashnikov and the concertina, they were both the tools of the devil, as far as he was concerned. He was now as convinced of the imminent coming of the Lord as he had been of the coming of the revolution and had no truck with distractions like music.

There was no death-bed recantation from Ewan MacColl. He was pretty well born into the Party and died in the Party. He never saw the revolution and, however long he had lived, never would have seen it, because it is not going to happen in any form that he would recognise. His legacy is not one of failure, however, because he left so many bloody good songs - the ones he wrote and the ones he revived. His brooding influence still permeates the folk scene.

I'll tell you something profoundly shocking about Ewan MacColl, though; more shocking than him winning a Song For Stalin contest, or attempting unsuccessfully to seduce a naïve English Rose. He claims in *Journeyman* that, when he opened up his first folk club in London, he was the only person through the door with a beard. Within a few years, it was possible to go to clubs where everyone, apart from some of the girls, either had a beard or was, like me, working on it. Now, that's what you call influence.

IF there really is such a thing as the Folk Police, perusing the scene and giving or withholding approval - and some surprisingly young performers regularly refer to it with nervous jokes - the temptation is to cast Ewan MacColl and A.L. Lloyd as Bad Cop and Good Cop. Unfortunately, it doesn't work very well as an analogy. Bert Lloyd was the other Big Beast in the primeval swamp of the early folk revival and, for all the vast difference in temperament and personality between the two men, they were essentially on the same side over the things that were important to them - music and politics; chalk-and-cheese allies rather than uneasy rivals.

I never had a curry with Bert Lloyd.

By reputation, it would have been just as illuminating as breaking naan bread with MacColl, but probably a rather jollier experience. Lloyd was a round, balding little man, with a strangely squeaky speaking voice. He had, by any standards, a varied and fascinating life. As a young man, he went from his home in London to Australia to work as a stockman. It happens that his first station was at Cowra in New South Wales, where I know some rugby league families - the Whatmores, the Simmonses and the Farrars - and where I have spent some time. Nobody remembers A.L. Lloyd, but the young Pom started a remarkable life's work there. It was in Cowra and at sheep-stations deeper into the outback where he subsequently worked that he began to collect songs. Back in Britain, he signed up for another seminal experience - a six-month voyage on an Antarctic whaler. The whalermen had a little band on board and their songs and style formed the basis of one of the best-loved folk albums of the Sixties - *Leviathan*. They also became staples in the repertoire of anyone who could wrestle a note out of a squeezebox.

One thing that Lloyd's traditional whaling songs had in common with his outback ballads was that there was an awful lot of A.L. Lloyd in them. The folklorists of Australia were angered by the informality of his approach; the would-be whalermen of Wallasey and points west did not much care.

It is not to belittle Lloyd's six months cutting up and boiling down blubber on a frozen deck to observe that he spent a lot more time singing about going to sea than he did actually going there. He wasn't an Australian farm-hand or an Antarctic whalerman. What he was most of the time was a journalist, who did much of his best work for *Picture Post*, under the editorship of Tom Hopkinson, who, much later, as the head of the journalism department at Cardiff University, was an invaluable guide and mentor to me as I tried to learn a few things about the craft.

What Bert Lloyd did retain over his working life ashore was a particular passion for songs of the sea; a show he put together called *The Seven Seas* includes in its set-list none other than 'The Rambling Sailor.' I don't think he messed around with that very much. He left that for me.

Consider, on the other hand, the fate of the itinerant harper, Glasgerion. In an old border ballad to which Lloyd took a fancy, the travelling musician knocks them dead at the castle and makes a date to meet the young countess in her bower. So far, so good; but his page gets wind of the tryst, impersonates his master and has his way with her under false pretences, although his rough and ready sexual technique should have been a clue. When Glasgerion finally turns up, she asks him whether he's back for more, the story comes out and the page is hanged. It's the sort of thing that must happen all the time to musicians on the road. The trouble was that Lloyd had no tune to go with the words, so he looked for one. And what would you think might be a suitable melody for this stirring tale of lust and betrayal? How about 'Donald, Where's Your Troosers?' Right first time; the affinity must be just too obvious. The tune of 'Jack Orion' - for that is the song it became - had always reminded me of something and now I know what it is. It also proved that the *I'm Sorry I Haven't a Clue* favourite, 'One Song to the Tune of Another' is a lot older than we thought. Carthy and Swarbrick did it to that tune and it seems a shame now that they never slipped in a verse to reveal the tune's guilty past. 'Jack Orion, Where's Your Troosers?' It has a certain ring to it.

It is one of many songs that we wouldn't have in any recognisable form if it wasn't for Bert's restorations and adaptations. Others that spring to mind are 'Reynardine' and 'The Two Magicians,' both of which seem to be largely his own work, although he always minimised his in-put. It makes a pleasant change to encounter someone who, instead of claiming authorship of something he did not write, denies authorship of something that he did. English folk music is full of his renovations, some of which have a rhythm and tone which, if you had to say what they don't sound like, the answer would be West European. This is no accident. Bert collected and recorded folk song in places like Bulgaria and Albania and that seems to have seeped into his other work, from sources closer to home.

Apart from this 'Balkanisation' of some unsuspecting English folk songs, the other way he influenced the direction of the revival was as an encourager and enabler of a younger generation. By stark contrast with MacColl, he could see the merits in applying electric instrumentation to traditional song. In his foreword to Dave Arthur's biography *Bert: The Life and Times of A.L. Lloyd*, Richard Thompson says that: '.....when we started electrifying old ballads and giving them a backbeat, Bert was one of the few figures from the folk establishment who was open-minded and supportive.'

Another fine singer, Louis Killen, puts it this way: 'Bert wasn't dogmatic at all, he was very erudite and we all appreciated that. If we wanted information, he'd supply it. He was very encouraging, he never laid down laws, like you've got to sing like this. As he said in a letter to me just before he died: "That was Ewan's job, what to sing, how to sing" ..... Bert was a stiletto man, distinct from MacColl who was a bludgeon man.'

Killen, second only to MacColl as a symbol of the bearded, belligerent face of folk, died at the age of 79 in 2013, but he died as Louisa Jo Killen, having undergone a gender reassignment. Meanwhile, Peggy Seeger was happily ensconced, on and off the stage, in a same-sex relationship. You couldn't write a song about it.

As for Bert Lloyd's sheer rock'n'roll credibility, though, how about this unlikely-sounding quote from that well-known folk song freak, Frank Zappa? 'When everyone else was listening to Cream, I was listening to A.L. Lloyd.' It's a marvellous thought.

For all his approachability and general likeability as a person, Lloyd does not completely escape the Shirley Collins hair-drier. In her interview in *FRoots* in 2012, she says this: 'Bert Lloyd could certainly handle a traditional song wonderfully, when he chose to, but otherwise there was always a sly twist, a slightly malicious or capricious grin, that I just found so irritating.'

Bert's records do include a fair bit of chuckling; some call it 'singing with a smile on his face.' I think the curry would have been fun. And now, over 30 years after his death, the little man in his half-moon glasses and Fair Isle sweater continues to have more influence on the way songs are performed than anyone - Ewan MacColl included.

Strolling Down the Highway: Bert Jansch and the Folk-Blues Guitar

ALONGSIDE all this rediscovery and reconstruction of British music, there was something quite different but parallel going on in the folk clubs, as often as not in the same room on the same night.

After the anti-virtuosity of the skiffle craze, the acoustic guitar didn't have much of an image. It was popularly supposed to be childishly easy to play three chords - badly. In those pre-Beatles days, the electric guitar meant The Shadows or Duane Eddy, but the acoustic was the runt of the litter. There were many reasons for going to what folk clubs there were in the early Sixties, but sitting watching someone playing a guitar all night was not one of them. You can mark down one guitarist and one tune that changed all that.

Davy Graham always came across as an exotic, cosmopolitan figure. In fact, he was born in Hinckley, Leicestershire, to a father from the Isle of Skye and a mother from Guyana, so that probably is pretty exotic. He was brought up in London, started playing the guitar at 12 and he was extraordinary - one of those musicians who re-invented an instrument and what it could do. He actually did invent a new guitar tuning to play music that fused blues, jazz and ideas he had picked up on his travels in North Africa and India. He was one of those musicians who sounded absolutely nothing like anyone who had gone before.

All of which begs the question of why, even among the enlightened readers of a book like this, there will be plenty who have never heard of him. There are lots of reasons for this state of affairs. He didn't exactly run his career with a shrewd business sense. He spent years in the grip of drugs and had a reputation for unreliability. There is a story about him being on his way to a booking at the Sydney Opera House - a pretty decent gig in anyone's book - but got off the plane in India to go and visit his sister in Goa instead.

He was signed to a major label - Decca - and they hadn't got a clue what to do with him. Was he jazz? Was he blues? Was he that mythical beast, the British Bob Dylan? They even seem to have laboured under the misapprehension that he was primarily a singer, which he never was in the memory of man. He had a perfectly pleasant voice, but instantly forgettable. You could never say that about his guitar-playing. Fifty years after he cut his best tracks, he still sounds cutting-edge. He could still go on something like Jools Holland's BBC show *Later* and make you say out loud 'What the hell is this?'

Although nobody had invented the horrible term at the time, he was a pioneer of world music. He crossed genres with no regard for the on-coming traffic - and with mixed results. He made a memorable album with Shirley Collins - yes, *that* Shirley Collins - which established early in the piece that the gap between the two major threads of what was going on in folk clubs - the folkies and the bluesers - was made to be bridged. He also recorded some of the weirdest covers of songs like 'Both Sides Now' and 'Don't Think Twice It's Alright' that you could wish to hear. He even did an instrumental interpretation of what he calls 'Ramblin' Sailor' which just needs someone talking a few lyrics to make it complete. Some of his recorded guitar work was eclectic in the extreme; you might easily have missed his pioneering abduction of Indian ragas. What you will have heard, unless you have spent your life hermetically sealed away from finger-style guitarists, is the party-piece that came to dominate the whole career of Davy (or Davey - he spelt it both ways) Graham.

Angi (or Angie, or Anji, or Anjie - spelling never was his strong point) was the girl who used to take the hat around whilst he was busking in his youth. When he put together two-and-a-half minutes of throw-away virtuosity that seemed to stop people in their tracks, he called it after her. 'Angie' - the tune, not the girl, who would be in her 70s by now and probably known for the last half-century as Angela - became a rite of passage among aspiring guitarists, a piece of music that made you think: 'If I work really, really hard at it, if I go down to the crossroads like Robert Johnson and sell my soul to the devil, I might just about be able to play that.' For the very best, the bar could be set a little higher. You could aim for a sort of über-Angie, with added twiddly bits; however difficult it was, you could make it a bit more so.

Bert Jansch had heard Graham's original before it was released, on an EP shared with Alexis Korner in 1961. He had got hold of a master-tape and was already experimenting with different directions in which he could take the tune. A product of the Scottish club scene, Jansch with a guitar was

Davy Graham and then some. A jaw-dropping version of 'Angie' was a key component of his first LP, along with the maudlin 'Needle of Death' and his original party-piece, 'Strolling Down the Highway.' In many ways, this track was the distilled essence of early Jansch. Like a lot of his songs, the lyrics are no great shakes; in fact, some of them are bilge: 'Strolling down the highway ..... I'm going to get there my way.' That gives you some idea - and it's one of his better couplets. Like Dylan, his singing is a moveable feast; it can be good, bad or indifferent. His guitar-playing, on the other hand, is from another planet. That first album, with its plain blue cover and moody portrait of a young man who already looked as though he had been through the mill, was passed from hand to hand like some sort of holy relic: 'You've got to hear this,' guitarists said - and you had. Part of the legend was that Bert didn't even own a guitar and had recorded that first LP on a borrowed instrument. I certainly saw him more than once arrive on stage empty-handed, simply pick up the nearest and play that. There were some who believed that the magic could be passed on that way; Jansch had that sort of mystique.

'Strolling Down the Highway' is a suitable starting-point, because it was an anthem to hitch-hiking, which was the way you got around at the time. It was the way I got to London to see Bert Jansch play. By this time, he was a regular on the Soho basement club scene, centred around a joint called Les Cousins, which was French for your uncle's kids, not the name of the man who ran it. I still had one mate from my primary school days in London - one who didn't try to kill me with bean-bags that day - and he had taken up the guitar. Barry Burton didn't look quite as frazzled by experience as Bert Jansch did, but life hadn't been straightforward for him. To me, he was just a mate, but my folks associated him with a chaotic home set-up. The give-away was the footwear; Wellington boots in summer, open-toed sandals or pumps in the snow. He generally used to go away from our flat with something different on his feet from what he had arrived in. His great ambition was to be a jockey, but he was handicapped by quite severe agoraphobia, which stopped him leaving his house for weeks at a time in later life. Funnily enough, he seemed able to cope with Soho by night, but he was never going to make it as a jockey until indoor horse-racing became the norm. His second choice of job would have been as a singer and guitarist. He wrote one he thought I would like, a type of calypso which went:

> 'Wigan.
> Wigan is the town for rugby.
> Wigan.'

It loses a bit in translation, but you have to remember that for Barry, trapped in his maisonette in Middlesex, Wigan was like the dark side of the moon. Surprisingly, he never made it as a singer-songwriter either, but we stayed in touch for years. He introduced me to all sorts of music; I introduced him to Wigan.

In our Soho days, what we would do was this. I would finish whatever Saturday job I had, or playing rugby for the school, and stick my thumb out at Junction 22 of the M6 at Lowton, near Leigh. Even on a slow day, I could guarantee being in Soho by midnight, which was plenty early enough. We would float around a few clubs, hear a bit of music - Bert Jansch if we were very lucky, one of the other, almost as technically accomplished players if not. Towards dawn, we'd get a train to Hayes, if there was one; if not, there was always a Salvation Army shelter or, on one occasion, a churchyard. In our dreams, we'd pick up a couple of rich American folkettes with a flat close by, but that didn't happen very often.

It all begs the question of what our parents were thinking about around this time. After all, they could go into a panic over your hair getting too long, but here we were wandering the streets of Soho at midnight without it raising any alarms. I might have forgotten to mention that part of our plans, but they knew how I got there. Hitch-hiking was just the way you got around in those days; it was taken for granted. I went to Keele largely because it was a motorway services with a university attached. Five minutes strolling across a farmer's field and you were at Hitchhike Central. A few more minutes and you were on your way to anywhere, north or south. Not only was it cheaper than the train, it was more convenient. A lot of the drivers who picked you up there expected some juicy anecdotes about free love and cheap drugs. Some of the tales I made up were so convincing that I finished up believing them myself.

My golden thumb took me a lot further afield than the M6 and Soho. It took me to Morocco, Greece, East Germany - tricky one, that - and all the way across North America. I only had one dodgy experience when a Turkish carpet salesman thought he deserved more than a thank-you and a firm handshake in return for a lift to Skopje. Apart from having to resolve that little misunderstanding, hitch-hiking served me well for many years, without any major dramas. There was that stolen car in Canada that the driver filled up from fuel tanks at remote farms, but that's a different story. As is the one about acting as a bodyguard for a Spanish portrait painter. Apart from that, no complications at all.

If one of my kids even mentioned the possibility of doing anything of the like now, I'd have nightmares for a month. Even with the benefit of 40-odd years of hindsight, it still seems an odd sense of proportion that I was turned loose regularly on the motorway network and in the big, wicked city, but it was alright as long as my hair was tidy. Mind you, my mum once dropped casually into the conversation that when she was 16 - and already a dead ringer for a young Ingrid Bergman - she travelled down to London on the back of her maths teacher's motorbike. I don't know what was going on there, but it makes my little adventures look like something straight out of the national curriculum.

Of course, you didn't have to hitch-hike to Soho to see Bert Jansch. He toured extensively and played in big concert venues as well as acrid basements. He never quite seemed comfortable on the concert stage, though. I recall one particularly shambolic evening at the Free Trade Hall, when he worked his way through a decanter of whiskey or brandy glinting at his right elbow. The chat between numbers became more and more rambling and mumbling; the vocals likewise. But, through it all, the guitar - his or someone else's - rang true, clean as a knife, never a bum note. To see him in a Soho cellar, though, was to see a man in his ecological niche.

His music branched out in all directions, notably towards the British and Irish traditional repertoire. One of his albums was called *Jack Orion*, with a nine-minute title track that owed little to Donald or his troosers. His version of 'Blackwater Side' must be the classic example of a new arrangement feeding back into the tradition, although to prove this you would have to set up rather a tricky controlled experiment. What you need is a particularly isolated Irishman or woman who has been singing 'Blackwater Side' for fifty years and has never heard Jansch's version. My contention is that they would still sing it with Bert's blues inflexions, because they have ingrained themselves so deeply into the song. And that's quite apart from inspiring Jimmy Page and Led Zeppelin's 'Black Mountain Side.' He was also responsible for the most frustrating piece of music of all time - a dazzling instrumental take on 'The First Time Ever I Saw Your Face' that lasts all of 1 minute and 12 seconds. He's just getting warmed up and he's gone. If he didn't fancy taking it any further, surely he could have just played it through again. After years of trial and error, I've found that I can achieve much the same effect by pressing the repeat button on my CD-player, but somehow it isn't quite the same. I did manage to persuade Sky TV to use it as my theme music when they made a film about my walk across the North of England. I smuggled in other bits and pieces from various Watersons and from Brass Monkey and I hope they all got the price of a pint when the royalties filtered through.

If ever there was an unlikely candidate to be a team player in a commercially successful group, it was Jansch, but that is what he did next. Along with a very nearly as famous guitarist in John Renbourn, the crystalline singer, Jacqui McShee, and a jazz bassist and drummer, he founded Pentangle. They did not have an easy birth; they played the Windsor Blues Festival in 1967 as an electric band and bombed. It was still seen as Jansch and his backing group and *Melody Maker* dismissed it with one sentence: 'Bert Jansch was dire.' Pentangle went away and re-thought their approach. When they re-emerged, it was with the multi-layered acoustic sound with which they became synonymous. It was one of those things that shouldn't have worked, but did. Jansch's guitar work should have been cluttered by another high-profile plucker, not to mention a jazz rhythm section. Jacqui McShee's vocals were pitched so dog-whistlingly high that she was effectively another instrument, rather than a conveyor of lyrics. It should have been a mess. Instead, it was one of those periodic phenomena, a folk group that you don't have to be a folk fan to like. On the stereograms of the late-60s and early-70s, it was the high-class background music of choice. They eventually lost their way and drifted into blandness, but that was after several highly successful albums - did anyone not have access to a copy of *Basket of Light*? - and years as a big attraction on the concert circuit. Post-Pentangle, both Jansch and Renbourn continued to pluck away in their particular directions; Renbourn into medieval and early music, Jansch into traditional music from both sides of the Atlantic and his own song-writing. One song that had a particular resonance was Renbourn's version of 'Lord Franklin' - previously filched by Bob Dylan - with Pentangle. It's a traditional song about a ship trapped in ice whilst looking for the North-West Passage around Canada; resonant because Renbourn and Jansch were the tip of an iceberg themselves.

By the time Pentangle broke up, there were virtuoso guitarists everywhere, guys like John James, Wizz Jones, Al Stewart, Gordon Giltrap and Stefan Grossman. The one who really hit the jackpot was Ralph McTell, thanks to that now utterly worn-out old warhorse, 'Streets of London.' He too started his performing career as a flash-Harry guitar-picker, first and foremost. They all owed a debt to bluesmen like Sonny Terry and Brownie McGee, who toured Britain extensively, Champion Jack Dupree liked it so much that he never went home, spending the rest of his life in Halifax.

Below the men with the national reputations in the league pyramid, there were the local guitar heroes, the part-timers who prided themselves on being the fastest gun in town.

In Bolton, it was Stu Butterworth - henceforward known as 'Spiderfingers'. He was Championship rather than

Super League, but he had a lot of things right. He could play a pretty gob-smacking version of 'Angie' with his own twiddley bits grafted on; variations on a theme by Graham and Jansch. What he was going to play it on was another issue. It could be a battered, borrowed six-string, a 12-string the size of a small wardrobe, or occasionally a gleaming, steel-fronted National, so loud that it rattled windows at the other end of Bradshawgate, especially when played in conjunction with a bottleneck. He wasn't much of a singer. He affected a Mississippi growl that rode roughshod over any notions of authenticity. Or, as the Bonzos posed the question: 'Can blue men sing the whites?' He couldn't. He was boorish and frequently pissed and, on a bad night, couldn't tune any guitar for toffee. When he had a woman in tow, he used to treat her mean and expect her to get the beers in.

Nor was Spiderfingers any oil painting to look at. He was going bald at a gallop and trying to grow his hair at the same time; the result was a greasy comb-over and retreating fringe that was part Bobby Charlton, part Van Morrison. The spider his fingers resembled was the rare nicotine spider. He'd a pock-marked complexion reminiscent of the dark side of the moon. He made me look handsome by comparison ..... but he could play 'Angie' - and that was his trump card. At one time, he and I both had an interest in a particular girl in the audience. Well, I say particular. We were probably both hoping that she wouldn't be too particular. (There were plenty of what my Australian friends would describe as 'good sorts,' charmingly referred to by Ewan MacColl as 'tit-hawkers,' in folk clubs in those days.)

It was no contest. I took her to see Carthy and Swarbrick at the Manchester Sports Guild, no small undertaking on the number 8 bus, but it was no good. She pined for Spiderfingers and his fancy fret-work. He had

'Angie' and, on a good night, a National Steel guitar; I had custody of a spotlight and a book of raffle tickets. If someone had fronted up who could play 'Angie' better, though, Spiderfingers would have been blown out as well, like a stag confronted by a bigger set of antlers.

The tune has had a life of its own. It has been played by A-listers like Paul Simon and Nick Drake and has been sampled by Chumbawamba. When Topic Records issued *Three Score and Ten*, a seven CD compilation to mark their 70 years in the business, side one, track two was 'Angi,' despite it being wholly atypical of their output. Like no other piece of music, it encapsulates a time and a place with complete precision. If, however, you want an actual song that does the same for this facet of the folk scene, I have to refer you to a performer who made only one album and sang only one song that anyone remembers. Welcome to the truly tragic world of Jackson C. Frank.

The song is 'Blues Run the Game.' They certainly ran Jackson C. Frank's game, because his life-story reads like a series of mishaps and misadventures that would give a saint the blues. From Buffalo, New York State, he suffered severe burns and almost died when his elementary school burned down, killing 18 of his class-mates. For a bluesman, it was one hell of a start in life.

He used his time in hospital to learn the guitar and, when he finally got his insurance settlement, blew a big slice of it on a luxury liner ticket to England. It was in mid-Atlantic that he wrote 'Blues Run the Game,' a song about exactly what he was doing, sailing into the unknown and putting your future in the hands of chance.

> 'Catch a boat to England, baby,
> Maybe to Spain.

Wherever I have been,
Wherever I've been and gone,
Wherever I have played,
The blues have run the game.'

In London, he shared a flat with Simon and Garfunkel - just imagine the queue for the bathroom - and was the boyfriend who persuaded Sandy Denny to give up her job as a nurse - bizarrely, a role she was to play in the film of The Who's *Tommy* - and sing full-time. He cut an LP, which became a cult favourite; the title track was a folk club staple, but nobody sang it like him. Not even Bert Jansch, whose version I have just watched on YouTube. It appears to have been filmed in a pub before opening time, but Bert has a pint to hand. It's great, but it's not Jackson C. Frank.

JCF should have been on his way to a modest level of stardom, but within the space of a few months, he got writers' block, stage fright and ran out of money. Back in America, his marriage broke up, his infant son died of cystic fibrosis and he booked himself into - and then escaped from - a mental institution. Just for light relief, he spent the next 20 years living on the streets of New York, resorting occasionally to psychiatric institutions when times got just too tough. He was sitting on the porch of a half-way house for mental patients when a gunman in a passing car shot him, blinding him in his left eye. You would think there was the material in all this for at least one more fatalistic classic, but it was not to be. Jack Frank, as he became known, had a few relatively stable years when he talked of writing again, but he died in 1999.

Davy Graham lasted until 2008, after living out his latter years in a fair degree of obscurity, teaching guitar in the West of Scotland. He got some air-time after he checked out - cult champions always do - and no doubt made a new generation of would-be guitarists go 'whoa.....' Richard Thompson devoted a verse of his song 'A Brother Slips Away' to him.

Bert Jansch carried on playing until shortly before his death in 2011. I head about it when I turned on Radio 4 in the morning. They did him proud, especially the high-profile business correspondent, Robert Peston, who turned out to be quite a fan.

Will we ever see their like again? Well, there seem to be more kids than ever toting guitars around, but this is one area in which I would take a lot of convincing that it could ever recapture all the innovative magic of the golden age of the folk-blues guitar. I'm ashamed to say that my instinctive, gut reaction when some new kid is touted as a successor and starts to get a bit big for his guitar-case, is to recall that famous put-down of a bumptious candidate who invoked an even more famous name during a US presidential election campaign. You know the one:

'Senator, I knew Jack Kennedy. Jack Kennedy was a friend of mine. Senator, you are no Jack Kennedy.'

For which I would substitute:

'Sonny, I saw Bert Jansch. Bert Jansch was a hero of mine. Sonny, you are no Bert Jansch.

'I'm not even sure that you're a Spiderfingers Butterworth, but keep on practising.'

If I hear something extraordinary from a guitar these days, the chances are that it is being used to accompany a song - often a traditional song. There is no shortage of invention in that department: Carthy still, Martin Simpson, Dick Gaughan, Kris Drever, recordings of Nic Jones before his car crash, Richard Thompson, of course, in a category of his own. And, just occasionally, you see and hear something you've never come across before.

Tim Edey is from Kent and plays guitar and squeeze-box in an acclaimed duo with New Zealand's leading harmonica player - I think I'm on pretty safe ground describing him as that - Brendan Power. Edey - no relation to Duane Eddy - is a wizard on both instruments, but whilst playing guitar on a set of tunes he did something I'd never seen. Still playing with his right hand, he used his left to unfasten and reposition his capo - the little device that clamps the strings to the finger-board - without breaking stride. He did it without any fuss, as though it was the logical way to change key in mid-tune. It wasn't quite Hendrix playing with his teeth or with his guitar behind the back of his neck - for a real challenge try both simultaneously - but I saw guitar-pickers in the audience turn pale. It was akin to watching someone change his tyre in the Tour de France, without bothering to stop his bike and dismount.

'Hmm.....' I fancy the aspiring guitarists in the Band on the Wall that night were thinking, 'this fellah's a bit different.'

Indeed he is; having read around the subject a little, it turns out that he has obsessive compulsive disorder. I don't mean to diminish the potential seriousness of that condition when I say that there are worse things for a finger-style guitarist to suffer from. I reckon some of us in the audience have got a dash of it as well.

Ireland: The Little House of Treasures Next Door or Just the Noisy Neighbours?

LET me ask you to consider these three cameos, which between them might just say something about the role of folk music in Ireland.

FOR starters, we are in a pub on a crossroads on the West Coast. I couldn't tell you just where. I couldn't even narrow it down to a county. Let's just say it was somewhere between Kerry and Donegal. We're waiting the statutory ten or 15 minutes for our pints of Guinness when, from the other little room, there is a familiar sound.

'Plunk-plunker-plunk,' it goes. 'Aha,' I think, 'banjo.'

'Plunker-plunker-plink-plunker-plunk.'

'Pretty tasty banjo,' we say.

And then an avalanche of plink and plunk, a torrent of notes that chase each other around the little pub, never quite catching up with the one in front, but nipping its heels.

'What the hell?' we say and stick our heads into the

side room. There, plinking and plunking away for the benefit of the five other customers, is an instantly recognisable figure. The thickset man with the heavy black beard, greying at temple and tash, is the most famous banjo-player in the world, Barney McKenna of The Dubliners. He plays a few tunes, shouts good-night and slips out.

'Sure, he likes to call in and play when he's passing,' says the barman.

When he's passing? Going from where to where? We're in the middle of nowhere.

'Well, you got here, didn't you?' he says, as he applies the finishing touches to the liquid sculpture that is a pint of Irish Guinness. 'You found us.'

FOR our second scenario, we aren't even in Ireland, but in a mock-Irish pub in Manchester - although it could be a mock-Irish pub anywhere in the world. The occasion is an evening with arguably the best fiddler in Irish music, Martin Hayes, and his guitarist, Denis Cahill.

Now, Hayes is a very particular type of Irish fiddler. He is not flash and brash like Frankie Gavin of De Dannan, for instance. His playing is subtle and reflective; gentle, quiet even. I know this because a young Irish harpy - as opposed to harpist - is just about standing on top of him, telling me and everyone else, at top volume, what a national treasure he is.

'Sure, the great thing about yer man is that you have to listen,' she bellows. 'I said you've got to feckin' listen. It's the keeping quiet and the feckin' listening you've got to do. Otherwise, you feckin' miss it. So you REALLY, REALLY need to listen!'

Somewhere in the background, Martin Hayes is playing a slow air, quietly.

FOR number three, I can tell you exactly where we are. We are in one of Dublin's major music pubs, O'Donoghues.

It's so packed that they are employing a Guinness-passer, a nimble old chap who stands on the bar, collecting the money and handing out the pints above the scrum. I'm wedged in a corner of the bar, with the stout production-line on one shoulder and a solid phalanx of fiddlers - four of them, knocking sparks off each other - cutting off any line of retreat. I can't go anywhere. Culturally as well as architecturally, I'm in my niche. Eventually, a couple of members of the rugby team I'm touring with notice that I'm missing from the main body of the raiding party. Don't worry about him, says another. He's in Hadfield Heaven.

IF you love the feel, the texture of Irish music, it isn't difficult to be in heaven; you don't even have to go anywhere near Ireland. No small nation has exported its distinctive music so successfully.

Take the American juggernauts of jazz, blues and rock out of the equation and no other country has spread its brand world-wide so effectively. You can go anywhere on the planet and hear the unmistakable strains of Irish music, not just in recorded form, but often played live by people who have never been within thousands of miles of the auld sod. It might be *Riverdance*; it might be a busker with a tin whistle, but the world has taken Irish music to its heart. It has got it, as my wife is wont to say, off Pat.

It started for me with The Dubliners, which meant that I more or less missed their pre-cursors, the Clancy Brothers and Tommy Makem. For a while, they were a global phenomenon as well and they continue to define one strand of the music - the big-voiced, hearty chorus-singing strand.

They were huge in the States, where a young Bob Dylan was surprisingly keen on them, and they were the only group always to wear the Arran sweaters that are often supposed to be synonymous with folk. They are a bit of a cautionary tale about the dangers of an unwise choice of a signature garment. A chunky sweater might have been suitable for draughty pubs and clubs in Cork or New York, but under the lights of a concert stage they must have sweated like pigs. It meant that for the latter stages of their career, the Clancys, quite literally, stank.

The Dubliners had a trademark of their own. They were, until the hirsute arrival of ZZ Top, the most whiskery group the world had seen. To one who had already made a prior commitment to beardedness, that made them very impressive. When, many years later, they had their first non-bearded member, he looked somehow naked among them on stage, as much so as if he had forgotten his trousers.

Their other defining feature was the singing of Ronnie Drew. He had a beard so heavy it seemed to be pulling the whole of his face down and a voice like a navvy's shovel scraped around a rusty gasometer. That is to say that it was a little on the rough side. There were pictures on the wall at O'Donoghue's commemorating the fact that The Dubliners were formed there and that was the sort of environment that suited them; nice and noisy and no need to shush the chatterers. Like a few other folk turns, they had a mainstream hit almost by accident, when Radio Caroline homed in on 'Seven Drunken Nights' on the Major Minor label and played it to death. If that was their major hit, they had a minor one with 'Black Velvet Band' and were a big attraction in the English-speaking world and beyond for years.

It's a fair bet, though, that everywhere they went already had an Irish music scene. Anywhere the Irish got to had one and in the pubs of North London and the bars of New York and Boston it was huge. I have sat in on Irish sessions in Brisbane and Auckland and you can't get much further from O'Donoghue's than that. The session is part of Ireland's musical legacy to the world. Typically, it consists of a circle or a half-circle of musicians on licensed premises; a variety of instruments, a variety of levels of expertise and preferably not more than one bodhrán, the Irish goat-skin drum. You kick a few tunes around, find one that everyone can have a stab at and off you go. It works well in some other musical cultures, but nowhere better than with the Irish, the expatriate Irish and the would-be Irish.

My first experience of it was in the Irish pubs of Manchester, where a group called the Beggarmen often seemed to be running the show. There was often a brilliant young banjo player called Sully and all manner of fiddle and squeezebox operators. And it wasn't just for those with Irish bloodlines. At similar sessions, in Birmingham and Leeds respectively, Dave Swarbrick and Barry Dransfield had honed their craft.

Irish music has never stopped giving. Its other source of strength was that it never stopped taking either. Like a jackdaw, it has always had an instinct for purloining the glittery things from other cultures that it took a fancy to. Take the banjo, for instance, as played by Messrs McKenna, Colluney and Sullivan; as Irish as you can get, right? Well, not really. It was brought to America and adapted by African slaves, played in Negro string-bands and the Minstrel shows that parodied them. When those shows toured Europe, the strange instrument with the distinctive 'plunk' was picked up everywhere, but it was in Ireland that it really found a new home - there and in Bluegrass and Old Timey music in the States and in Trad Jazz.

Take the even more surprising journey of the bouzouki. The classic stringed instrument of the tavernas of Greece, it was brought to Ireland by Johnny Moynihan of the group, Sweeney's Men, in the mid-60s and it was almost instantly assimilated. Influential figures like Andy Irvine and Dónal Lunny took it up and, before long, you could hardly have a proper-job Irish band without one. It was no whim; it was just the ideal rhythm instrument for Irish music. No wonder that there soon seemed to be more bouzoukis in Athlone than in Athens.

The Irish didn't steal the harmonium, but they found it. To be precise, they found a tune called 'Music for a Found Harmonium' and made it their own. Originally, it was nothing to do with folk or Ireland. Simon Jeffes, the leader of the Penguin Café Orchestra, wrote it when he quite literally found a harmonium dumped in a back-street in Kyoto, where he was living at the time. His composition, as far as he was concerned, fell into a genre called Chamber Jazz, if it fell into any category at all. As soon as the Irish heard it, though, they said: 'We're having that.'

And they did. It just transformed beautifully into a reel, especially one that performs that favourite Irish party-trick of getting faster and faster. Within a few years it was an Irish standard, recorded by the likes of Four Men and a Dog, Patrick Street and Sharon Shannon, just to concentrate on the top of the first division. Plenty of bog-standard bands have given it a kicking as well. It's the biggest cliché in Irish music and it isn't even Irish.

It is evidence, however, that just about any tune can be Irishified. The leading practitioners of this are undoubtedly De Dannan. They will take anything from mainstream classical to mainstream pop and make it sound as though it was born and bred in Donegal. Try their version of 'Hey Jude,' for instance, or a whole album of chart covers, wittily entitled *Welcome to the Hotel Connemara*. And does it include 'Bohemian Bloody Rhapsody?' I hear you ask. Yes, of course it does.

At the other end of their repertoire, De Dannan were responsible for the music at our wedding, 'The Entry of the Queen of Sheba.' Or at least, they were responsible for taking Handel's early bumbling attempt and turning it into the Irish tune it was always meant to be. As the guests settled into their pews at Bank Street Unitarian, they were treated to a rendition of 'Tabhair Dom Do Lámh,' which translates as 'Give Me Your Hand.'

All this Irishness had less to do with Ruth's tenuous Irish links - something about the Spanish Armada being wrecked off the West Coast of Clare - than with my taste in music at the time. In fact, I'd launched a determined search for the Irish relatives I felt confident I ought to have. No luck though; the closest I could come up with was Great Uncle Frank, my mum's cousin's dad, and he was an Orangeman and that wasn't the same thing at all. But Irishness is a flexible concept.

You can listen to a polka played on accordion, banjo and bouzouki and think 'Yes, Irish,' but what you're actually hearing is a Polish tune played on instruments originally from Germany, West Africa and Greece. So don't tell me what's Irish and what isn't. I might be as Irish as a bouzouki-maker in Piraeus, but I had a big, fat Irish wedding. The day after I was made an honest man of, we went to see The Chieftains in Blackburn and they played 'Tabhair Dom Do Lámh' for us. I didn't have the heart to tell them that we'd actually used Planxty's version.

The Chieftains and Planxty were the opposite poles of Irish traditional music, completely different in just about every respect. That includes their longevity, with Planxty shooting across the sky like a shining but short-lived comet and The Chieftains apparently eternal. They did have one thing in common, though; the prominence of the world's most under-rated musical instrument - the uilleann pipes. I first heard the pipes in the hands of Paddy Maloney on the early Chieftains albums, the ones you could only get on Irish labels. It was Jeff Lowe who played them to us as part of our singing lessons. I couldn't see the precise relevance, how a wholly instrumental LP was going to help me sing 'The Rambling Sailor' in tune, but I sure as hell loved the sound of those pipes. They look like an instrument designed by a committee, a near-random collection of bag and bellows, drones and chanter. They are as temperamental as a display cabinet full of banjos and have the wild sound of an animal about to snap its leash and go on the rampage.

They are also the great survivors of the bagpipe family. At one time, everywhere in Europe had its native version of the pipes. The notable ones that still thrive are the Scots bagpipes, the Northumbrian small-pipes, the ones they play in Galicia and elsewhere in Northern Spain, some in France - and the uilleann pipes of Ireland.

Paddy Maloney also messes around with various whistles, but his pipes are the dominant sound of The Chieftains; a sound which has taken them many times around the world. Having long ago exhausted the possibilities of playing Irish music in an Irish style, their last couple of decades have been largely devoted to collaborations with assorted partners, likely and unlikely. One of the most successful was one of the least obvious, *The Chieftains in China*; some others have made me wonder how long it can be before we have 'The Chieftains Meet Take That.' Most original members have retired or died, but still at the heart of it are Maloney and his pipes. Somewhere in the thousands of hours of music he has made on them is the key to singing 'The Rambling Sailor.'

If The Chieftains are effectively Ireland's national folk orchestra, then Planxty had the attitude and impact of a rock band. Unlike The Chieftains, they majored on two great singers, Andy Irvine, and - last seen guesting for a fiver a night in Bolton - Christy Moore. Their instrumental line-up was completely different as well; an assortment of stringed things, including guitars, mandolin, mandola and sometimes two bouzoukis. The only meeting point was the pipes, played in Planxty by Liam O'Flynn, who was, for my money, responsible for two of the most magical moments in Irish - or any other - music. On the group's first album, he leads them through a segue from 'The Raggle-Taggle Gypsies' to 'Tabhair Dom Do Lámh' - yes, our old favourite again - that makes you want to stand up and cheer. You can hear something similar happen on their reunion album, *Planxty: Live 2004*. This starts with an instrumental set appropriately called 'The Starting Gate.' It's going along quite merrily with O'Flynn on the whistle - a treat in itself - but the audience is waiting for something else. He puts that instrument aside and starts building up the air pressure in his pipes. You can hear a faint drone behind the continuing music as he does it, plus a buzz from the crowd. Then he's off and away and the audience are on their feet whooping, just as they did in the heyday of the band 30 years earlier, or in their first revival, when I saw them at the Manchester Apollo in the 80s. They do the same on that album with 'Raggle Taggle Gypsy,' to the same effect. In fact, every time Liam O'Flynn flexes his elbow on his bellows the crowd goes mental. For sheer generation of excitement, only the Bothy Band, another even more short-lived Lunny project with Paddy Keenan on pipes, came close.

All of which raises the question of why Planxty ever left the pipes out of the mix at all. After all, if you had George Best in your side, wouldn't you want to pass the ball to him all the time, not merely most of it? I sometimes think there's a system of rationing going on here, a decision not to give you what you want all the time, on the grounds that it wouldn't be good for you. It felt like that in the case of the McGarrigles, who occasionally seemed as though they were doling out the transcendent harmonies you had come for rather parsimoniously. The same applies to another pair of sisters, The Unthanks.

For all the other great stuff they do, what you really want is to hear Rachel and Becky singing together. You get it too, but, oh, they make you wait - sometimes for a whole two numbers.

The most outrageous example of this was in the band to which Planxty passed the baton, Moving Hearts. Not only did they have a dynamic and innovative piper in Davy Spillane, they also had the unique selling point of the alto sax of Keith Donald. The two instruments are not obvious partners, but when they are played together they sound sensational. Perhaps wisely, the musicians' co-operative that was Moving Hearts limited the availability of that heady mix; it would have been too much for the listening public. A study of the use of the saxophone in folk music would amount to a fairly slim volume - not forgetting Lol Coxhill's work with Shirley Collins - but this was an insight into just how potent some unexpected combinations can be.

My nomination for the most exciting Irish music since Moving Hearts went their separate ways - Christy Moore to his hugely successful solo career - would be the accordion of Sharon Shannon. You might think that we are back on familiar Irish ground with the accordion, but it was invented in Germany in the 1820s and is another of those instruments co-opted by traditional musicians, for the simple reason that it works. In a country where skilled local musicians still exist in astonishing profusion, the village virtuoso is as likely to be a squeezebox player as a fiddler or anything else. When she first emerged, a shy slip of a girl from the West Coast playing up a storm, it was another of those times when people took a deep breath and said 'What on earth have we got here?' Not only was she outstanding in the conventional sense, she was a restless innovator. She played with The Waterboys, with hip-hop and dub producers, with Steve Earle on his song 'Galway Girl,' which became Ireland's top-selling track and - an even more glittering prize - the music for a Guinness advert. And she isn't even from Galway, but from Co. Clare. That folk-geography thing again.

Sharon is largely responsible for one of the best all-round days of my life. I'd better clarify that. What I'm talking about is a day that has at least two unconnected (and printable) highlights. This one had Great Britain beating Australia at rugby league at Wembley, a few gloating pints in Earls Court, a great feed in the Edgware Road's only Burmese restaurant and Sharon Shannon and band at Shepherd's Bush Empire. It was, as my grandchildren would say, too much fun. The only day I can think of in England that comes close is the one that included lunch at the River Café, Leigh RMI getting a draw in the FA Cup at Premier League Fulham and Márta Sebestyén on the South Bank. A particularly good day if you have a bit of a thing about the Thames. And the soundtrack would be Ewan MacColl's 'Sweet Thames Flow Softly,' sung, as he did with Planxty, by Christy Moore.

A day in Hadfield heaven, for sure, but Shaz just shades the vote, because Ireland, at the end of the day, matters a bit more to me than Hungary. Anyway, the

Woodchoppers, as her band were known at the time, were on fire that night and Ms Shannon seemed to be having the time of her life, not just on the squeeze box but also in some mouthwatering double-fiddle stuff with one Mary Custy.

The next time I saw her was without the benefit of a great sporting upset as the warm-up act, but with an even bigger band, which featured a song or two from what looked like the ghost of Shane McGowan, plus a lad who seemed to have been brought along just to sing 'Galway Girl.' Between them, they repeatedly threatened to lift the roof off the Manchester University Students' Union.

By contrast, the next time was in a small venue that didn't seem to have let anyone who wasn't a blood relation know and I watched most of a largely solo performance with her sisters and aunts, who were numerous enough that they at least created the illusion of the place being full if they moved around regularly. As for me, I don't know which of the three gigs I enjoyed the most.

I can't imagine the accordion being played any better; but what, I hear you ask, of that other Irish stalwart, the flute? Not the overly-gentrified flute of James Galway - although I understand that he could probably manage a few proper-job Irish tunes if he put his mind to it - more like the flute of Matt Molloy in the Boys of the Lough and The Chieftains.

Or the flute as played by Dee Havlin. I have to declare an interest here. Dee is not only an All-Ireland flute champion and a member of the group, the London Lasses, she is also a friend and occasional flute-tutor to my youngest daughter. We first met at the funeral of a mutual friend. It was not a doleful occasion and most of us were okay until her heart-rending playing of 'Flowers of the Forest.' Then the tears flowed and catharsis was achieved.

She gave Sophie a few lessons and we spent some

days with her on the North Antrim coast near the Giants' Causeway. One night, Dee led a session in a pub in Portrush and Sophie was able to hang around the fringes and get the flavour of the thing. The actual notes played are one aspect; the other is the craic, the hard-to-define spirit of the whole business. Sometimes, I suspect, the craic makes the playing sound a bit better than it actually is, but I still reckon that there is more music per head of population in Ireland than anywhere I've been, with the possible exception of Cuba.

I wouldn't want to give the impression that it's an unblemished musical paradise. There is bad music in Ireland; they usually call it country and western. But fresh and vital music in the traditional idiom is everywhere, something illustrated nicely on the Saturday night we were there, when Dee, her flute and various accompanists were booked to play at not one, but three weddings, necessitating some speeding and swerving down the back-lanes of Antrim.

There had to be a future in this for a young flautist and her dad, you would think. It is not, however, all good times and laughs being a flute-father - the equivalent of a soccer mom. There were all those nights at the Deane Music Centre, wondering whether her teacher would dig his way through the snowdrifts on the Pennines. Most infamously, there was the time she left her rather expensive flute on the bus. A mate of mine, who has had every possible problem with his daughter, noticed that I was looking even more grumpy than usual and asked what was wrong. I told him the story of the lost flute. 'Dave,' he said. 'I can't tell you how I long to have that sort of problem.' Fair play to the man and fair comment without a doubt.

We got the flute back. She doesn't seem to actually play it all that often, but it's there on her shelf in Lincoln, along with a half-sized accordion and an ocarina. An ocarina, for heaven's sake, an instrument so obscure that I can think of only one CD on which it figures. Not strictly Irish either, of course, although its name makes it look as if it could be, especially if you adopt the alternative spelling as the O'Carina.

All in all, I remain hopeful that she could yet turn out to be the Irish relative I've been looking for all these years.

Folk-Rock:
The Music That Read its Own Obituary

I MUST have been a piss-poor purist, not to mention a bad, sad traddy, because the first time I heard the music that was to become known as folk-rock, I fell head-over-heels for that as well.

We have to tread the treacherous territory of definitions here. What you mean by the term folk-rock depends on where you were and when. Was it born when Bob Dylan plugged in at the Newport Folk Festival? Or when the Byrds applied their jangly guitars to folk songs? In Ireland, it was probably Sweeney's Men. For me, it was when Dave Swarbrick joined Fairport Convention.

My agoraphobic mate in London, close to being a full-time hermit by this stage, had been telling me how good Fairport were. He played me their first two albums without them knocking me sideways. 'Barry,' I told him. 'You need to get out more.' It was perfectly pleasant, but essentially a North London take on what was happening on the West

Coast of the United States, with covers of songs by Dylan and Joni Mitchell, although with their own song-writing coming increasingly to the fore. They sounded good, in an early London Underground type of way, but nothing ground-breaking.

All that was to change as the band – and bassist Ashley Hutchings in particular - started to display more and more symptoms of the folk virus. Sandy Denny, a child of the folk clubs, came in on vocals and there were two traditional songs on their second LP. The real breakthrough, though, came during the making of their third album, *Unhalfbricking*.

Swarb, already well-known from his partnership with Martin Carthy and disillusioned with the narrow-mindedness of the folk scene, was brought in to play some fiddle over-dubs on one track, but finished up playing on another four, including the epic 'A Sailor's Life.' Among the other tracks was what would be many people's choice as Denny's finest song, 'Who Knows Where the Time Goes?' As part of my guerrilla campaign to get this music into places it has no business being, I managed to quote extensively from it in an article for the official Australian guide to the 2012 Olympics. You can't keep a good song down. Equally notable was the inclusion on the album of Fairport's only chart single, 'Si Tu Dois Partir,' which was simply a French translation of Dylan's 'If You Gotta Go,' performed for a laugh in vaguely Cajun style. When they appeared on *Top of the Pops*, Ashley Hutchings played a giant double bass with a French loaf, Richard Thompson played accordion, their roadie looked after percussion whilst the drummer, Dave Mattacks, was on washboard. Most of the band wore rather natty French berets. There was some suspicion that they were not taking it terribly seriously, but they had enjoyed their statutory accidental hit.

Mattacks was on board because of the death in a

motorway crash after a gig in Birmingham of Fairport's original drummer, Martin Lamble. Also killed was Jeannie 'The Tailor' Franklyn, a clothes designer on the underground scene. For a while, the surviving members of the group considered disbanding, but *Unhalfbricking* was finished and released to considerable acclaim.

The recruitment of Mattacks meant that the line-up was in place for the biggest and best Fairport album, *Liege and Lief*; a sort of Team of All the Talents. The keynotes of what was already the band's fourth line-up were Denny's sublime vocals and the interplay of Thompson and Swarbrick's guitar and fiddle. That second element of their characteristic sound was not easily achieved. There was no such thing as an electric fiddle, so they created one by taping a telephone handset to the instrument and fed it straight into the amp. Contrary to the popular myth, it did not make Swarb go deaf in his left ear; he was already deaf and, for a time, it suited him to play electrically, because he could hear that when he couldn't hear a conventional violin. In the end, he paid the price, because he finished up really, really deaf.

I have always thought that I saw the great Fairport line-up's first gig and that it was either at Manchester or Salford students' union. According to Patrick Humphries, however, in his book *Meet on the Ledge: A History of Fairport Convention*, that debut was at Van Dike's Club in Plymouth - and I'm absolutely sure I never went there. They must have played Manchester (or Salford) soon after; certainly before *Liege and Lief* was released, because one thing I can remember is how completely new and radical it sounded. According to Humphries, the band were extremely nervous about how their new direction - fundamentally all about electrifying traditional material - would be received. They need not have worried; if Salford (or Manchester) was in any way typical, it went down a storm. From memory, their equipment wasn't great and the balance wasn't always perfect, but it worked a treat on a very visceral level. Quite simply, unless they'd been at Plymouth a couple of nights earlier, nobody had heard the native rhythms of these islands played at that volume. Throw in the Thompson-Swarbrick chemistry and, floating above it all, the voice of Sandy Denny and it was irresistible. A gang of us had gone together. We missed the last bus, we missed the last train; we walked the 12 miles back to Bolton, slowing down only for fish and chips in Kearsley.

That line-up and that album defined folk-rock. They showed what you needed; you had to have a bass and drums, at least one virtuoso lead instrument, a voice of distinction and songs and tunes plucked from the tradition. Other templates appeared later, but in 1969 this was the formula - and it grabbed the attention of a public well beyond the reach of folk music previously. *Liege and Lief* sold like no folk album before or since. Sandy Denny was voted the *Melody Maker*'s top British female singer two years running - and this, of course, in all genres, not just the mysterious backwaters of folk-rock.

And then, as soon as they seemed to have got it right, it all started to break up. In this order, Sandy left because it was too folky, Ashley Hutchings left because it wasn't folky enough and Richard Thompson left because he wanted to concentrate on being Richard Thompson, something he has done to great effect ever since. He rides off into the sunset at this point and into a chapter of his own.

He was still on board for *Full House*, a good enough album in its own right, apart from its failure to tackle the question of who was going to do the singing. Both Thompson and his fellow founder-member, Simon Nicol, were reticent about stepping up to the microphone. The surprise, coming up on the rails, was Dave Swarbrick. Never allowed to as much as join in with a chorus during his years with Martin Carthy, he suddenly emerged as the lead vocalist in the biggest folk band in the country. As he would admit, he had his vocal limitations, but there was pleasure to be had in hearing him work his way around them. 'Hang on,' I thought more than once. 'He's sort of talking this. I wonder if he knows "The Rambling Sailor".'

Patrick Humphries' excellent 1982 history of Fairport includes one of Pete Frame's famous Rock Family Trees - headlined 'Resolving the Fairport Confusion' - and the best way of following their subsequent career is to refer to that. Frame identifies 15 different line-ups until they officially folded in 1979, including such twists and turns as a near two-year return by Sandy Denny. As a band with a revolving stage-door and a constantly changing cast of characters, it was inevitable that their output could best be described as uneven. Buy a ticket for a Fairport gig and you were never quite sure who you would be seeing - or what state they would be in. There were times when they were too drunk to play properly; although not as drunk as Kevin Ayers and the Whole World when I once saw them literally incapable of standing. They played a whole set lying on the stage and nobody thought it was particularly untoward.

On the other hand, there were certain times and certain line-ups that could still produce invigorating performances, both live and on record. They were worth the risk and I saw them when I could; sometimes the best way to enjoy them to the max was to be pretty steaming yourself. They were a good-time band, with echoes of tragedy - Martin Lamble and, in 1978, Sandy - reverberating in the background.

They finally knocked it on the head in 1979....or tried

to. Swarb, by this time, had very serious hearing problems, although not as serious as the *Daily Telegraph* was to imply a couple of decades later. He had, in his idiosyncratic way, held it together over the previous few years and to carry on without him did not look viable. Within a year of breaking up, however, they were back together for the first of their innumerable reunions at Cropredy in the North Oxfordshire countryside. The following year's event was at nearby Broughton Castle, before it put down permanent roots - or so it seems - in the village that has become synonymous with Fairport nostalgia.

I started going to Cropredy in 1983, sometimes taking the family, sometimes a posse of non-folky workmates. One year, I had to break away on the Saturday afternoon to cover a match at Coventry City. Another year, I was on crutches with a leg in plaster and, by the time I got back from the chemical toilets at the top of the field, it was time to set off again. It was always a hoot. They had their system worked out; a couple of days of build-up, preferably including what ex-members were up to, then a marathon closing set by Fairport present and past and a feeling of bonhomie that I have never known matched. The test of quality nostalgia is that people who weren't even there first time around get all dewy-eyed as well. As a festival, it was big enough, but not too big; and, inevitably with Fairport, the beer - from Wadworth's of Devizes - was always good.

As an extinct band, they now seemed to have more fans than in their heyday, so the attraction of once more becoming a full-time entity - or as full-time as other commitments allowed - was hard to resist. Swarb's left ear could survive a few hours of electric fiddle in a field in Oxfordshire once a year, but not a full tour, so they brought in a new fiddler in Ric Sanders. Or should I say, a new violinist? Fun as it was at Cropredy, I couldn't really warm to Fairport without Swarbrick. He was just my idea of what a fiddler - especially in an electric folk band - should be. The new bloke might have been his technical equal, but to me he didn't sound like a fiddler. He sounded like a violinist. So did Peter Knight in Steeleye Span, which might ultimately have limited my enjoyment of them. Don't ask me to define the precise difference. The same instrument can do both jobs; maybe the distinction is largely in my head.

Jon Boden is a fiddler, so is Eliza Carthy; Barry Dransfield is a fiddler, who sometimes, just to be provocative, plays like a violinist; Nigel Kennedy is a violinist who occasionally plays like a fiddler.

Whenever the remnants of a band continue to milk it, you wonder about the provenance of what is being put before you, about the authenticity of the experience. I was once on holiday and went to see what purported to be The Drifters. Call me pernickety, but two of them were white. At least Fairport have been spared the ultimate indignity of multiple identities. There has never, to the best of my knowledge, been more than one Fairport Convention at any given time.

And so the show goes on - and good luck to them. Just as long as nobody kids themselves that they are seeing the real thing. To do that, you had to be at Manchester (or Salford) that Tuesday (or was it Wednesday) night in 1969. Or even at Plymouth, although that would have been a longer walk home.

Dave Swarbrick went back to playing acoustic fiddle around the folk clubs, often with Simon Nicol. He also had a series of other bands, the name of one of which, Lazarus, carried special significance for him with its biblical reference to rising from the dead.

On April 20 1999, the *Daily Telegraph* carried a half-page obituary of the leading instrumentalist in the folk revival and the world of folk-rock. They did him proud:

> 'A small, dynamic, charismatic figure, "Swarb" - cigarette perched precariously on his bottom lip, unruly hair flapping over his face, pint of beer ever at hand - could electrify an audience with a single frenzied sweep of his bow. He never failed to produce a dramatic effect, whether on fiddle or mandolin, whether playing in tiny folk clubs or at huge open air festivals.'

The only snag with this glowing tribute was that Swarb was sitting up in bed, on the mend in hospital in Birmingham, reading it. Like Mark Twain, reports of his death had been somewhat exaggerated. Or like Cider Billy, the local vagrant whose demise I once reported for my evening paper.

'There's someone down here complaining about the article,' the girl on the front counter told me. 'His name? Yes, it's a Mr Cider Billy.'

It could never happen to a violinist, only to a fiddler, and it would take a stronger man than me to resist the multi-decked symbolism of it. You have the English traditional music, which was supposed to have died, but which lives on. You have the folk-rock way of interpreting it, which was supposed to be a passing fad, soon to expire, but which is still very much a going concern. And then you have one of the prime movers in the whole business, chuckling over his breakfast as he reads of his death.

Mind you, in Swarb's case, it was an understandable mistake. He was a lot less healthy than many people who do die. He suffered from emphysema, not helped by the ever-present fag dangling from his mouth as he played. He had a double lung transplant and, for a while in the new millennium, performed from a wheelchair, hooked up to an oxygen cylinder. He couldn't even attempt to sing any more, but remarkably he could still play. What is more, he turned the clock back the best part of half a century by touring again with Martin Carthy. An old mate, who had spent forty of those years in Canada, managed to time a visit home so that he could see folk's Odd Couple play. One of his English memories was seeing their 'farewell' appearance - or was it a reunion? - around 1970. 'Gee,' he said admiringly, 'nothing changes around here.' How can it when old folkies simply refuse to die when they are supposed to?

Back in Fairport, Ashley Hutchings had latched onto traditional music with what Joe Boyd, their manager and producer called 'the zeal of a convert.' He said that Sandy, in particular, had been traumatised 'to suddenly discover that, having gotten into the rock'n'roll business, she was now in the same band as someone who was fast becoming almost as doctrinaire about British traditional music as all those people she had fled folk from.' Hutchings wanted to delve deeper in the direction pioneered on *Liege and Lief*; the trouble was that he needed a different band in which to do it. That band was Steeleye Span, an outfit whose early months make even Fairport seem uncomplicated.

The first-line up consisted of him, plus the all-Irish quartet of Terry and Gay Woods, Andy Irvine and Johnny Moynihan; there must have been plenty of bouzouki action there. They rehearsed, but never gigged, never had a name and never recorded. The latter two Irish luminaries departed for Planxty and in came Tim Hart and Maddy Prior, already an established duo on the club scene. This line-up, christened Steeleye Span after a character in the Lincolnshire song, 'Horkstow Grange,' thus guaranteeing a lifetime of confusion with Steely Dan, recorded an interesting album, *Hark, the Village Wait*, with a title that meant nothing to almost anyone, but never played live. That was left for the next manifestation of Hutchings' vision, minus Mr and Mrs Woods, but plus Peter Knight on fiddle and, on electric guitar for the first time, Martin Carthy. Getting such a legendary figure from the world of acoustic music to plug in seemed as radical as anything that had ever happened on the folk scene. It was something you had to experience.

So it was off to the students' union in Manchester (or Salford) to see how it all worked out. Now this, I'm as sure as I can be, really was their debut gig; they hadn't sneaked in one in Plymouth. It certainly seemed like a first gig, although their battered equipment, some of it held together with gaffer-tape, looked as though it had been on several world tours, mainly in the cargo holds of tramp steamers. It seemed to take an age to get everything working and get on stage; when they did, they had plenty of feedback problems and tuning issues that twanged on interminably, ensuring that by the time they finished playing the last bus would be long-gone and the chippy in Kearsley would be closed.

Beneath all the chaos, however, there was something just as exciting as that first (or second) Fairport gig. I don't think Carthy was ever at ease with the electric guitar or satisfied with the way he played it. To my ears, though, it made a pretty marvellous sound, something that can be confirmed by a quick listen to the two Steeleye albums on which he appeared before going solo again. Another sure-fire winner was him singing with Maddy. Somewhere, I have a cassette I made of the two of them singing around a campfire at some festival around 1970 (Norwich? Lincoln?) and they were born to harmonise together. Not only did he leave, though, so did Hutchings - this time to start the profusion of

Albion Bands which he has led. As the Albion Country Band, they joined forces with his then-wife, Shirley Collins, to make the third great folk-rock album - after *Liege and Lief* and Steeleye's *Please to See the King* - *No Roses*. There was the Albion Dance Band and the plain old Albion Band. There is even an Albion Christmas Band, or there is in December, at any rate.

Ashley Hutchings' track record is not that of a blinkered purist. He has done some hugely innovative things, but he would not have been comfortable in the next variant of Steeleye Span - the one that achieved all the commercial success - any more than he would have been in a boozy, laddish latter-day Fairport.

Steeleye had the requisite accidental chart hit with 'Gaudete,' sung unaccompanied in Latin and unrelated to the rest of their repertoire. 'All Around My Hat' was an even bigger hit and their albums and concert tickets sold by the truck-load. They were produced for a time by the pop svengali, Mike Batt, and their 'can't get more mainstream than that' moment came when four of them wore Womble costumes for a rendition of 'Remember You're a Womble' on *Top of the Pops*. Sadly neither Ewan MacColl nor Ashley Hutchings were in the studio audience that night.

Even allowing for that, there has been much to like about Steeleye. They introduced more people than anyone to the possibilities of British traditional music - more than Fairport, for sure and made it accessible to any but the most ardent ethnophobe. Maddy Prior was and remains a masterful singer, although not one to arouse the fierce devotion of Sandy Denny. Peter Knight sometimes attacked his violin with enough grunt to be reclassified as a fiddler. The tensions between their folk roots and middle of the road commerciality were always there, however, and eventually they pulled them apart, although not in a final or complete sense, and not before an intriguing little Indian summer, which saw a brief return by Carthy, who brought squeezebox guru John Kirkpatrick with him. Suddenly, they had their folk cred back. Like Fairport, they have been through all manner of permutations since. One line-up that claimed to be Steeleye Span consisted of Peter Knight and two bass-players. Both venerable folk-rock institutions live on, even if on a part-time, ad hoc basis. The genre as a whole also seems equipped to survive. I went to a beer festival in Dewsbury recently and the entertainment on the first night was provided by a band called Blackstone Edge - drums, bass, guitars and a manic fiddler - and they went down like free ale. They are building on a new tradition, but a tradition none the less.

When I think of highlights in the story since Fairport got stuck into 'A Sailor's Life,' I find I have to range rather far afield. There was Five Hand Reel, Scotland's finest, led by the redoubtable Dick Gaughan. In Australia, I naturally became a devotee of the Bushwackers, a sort of rocked-up outback combo who were as good fun as anything could be. The first time I saw them, at Kensington Town Hall in Sydney, the poster included the magical initials BYO - bring your own beer, wine or whatever. The local bottle shops were overwhelmed by the demand as music-lovers staggered off to the gig carrying blocks of 24 cans or bottles.

Now, that was a band that made you thirsty, just like long-haul flights made cricketer David Boon thirsty.

Back in Britain, some of the most fruitful, although rarely commercially successful, work has been written afresh, but in the folk-rock idiom. The Dransfield brothers had an electric band called, amazingly, Dransfield. Bob and Carol Pegg gave birth to Mister Fox, and Little Johnny England carried the sound and the attitude of folk-rock into the new millennium. The two most significant bands to pick up the beat, however, found new directions of their own.

The Home Service were a spin-off from one of the early Albion Bands, via various National Theatre productions. In terms of sheer manpower on stage and their use of a brass section, they were the precursors of Bellowhead. Like them, they were fronted by one of the great, distinctive voices of folk; in the Home Service's case, that of John Tams, who, amongst many other things, was responsible for the music in the TV series, *Sharpe*. I never saw them first time around, before the economic and logistical nightmare of keeping a football-team sized folk band on the road put paid to them.

I did see their reunion, though, as you can so often in this music if you miss something first-up. There was an epic quality about them and a sense of occasion that demonstrated that, without the Home Service, the range of what can be done in this genre would be that much narrower.

Another unique position in the whole story is occupied by the Oyster Band, or rather by Oysterband as they now style themselves. In fact, they were known as Fiddler's Dram when they had their inadvertent hit record with 'Day Trip to Bangor' - it was supposed to be Aberystwyth, but that didn't scan. The singer on that single, Cathy Lesurf, left to join another version of the Albion Band and the remaining members reverted to being what they had been before their brief brush with fame - which was essentially a céilidh band. What couldn't have been predicted was what they would develop into. They took beefed-up treatments of traditional songs and tunes as their starting point, but they were soon writing material with an anthemic sweep rare in any type of music.

If their albums packed a punch, their live performances are something else. If you are familiar with their back-catalogue, it's one show-stopper after another, except that the show doesn't stop; it never even pauses for breath. Until the advent of you-can-guess-who, their sheer power and pace made them the most consistently uplifting live act in the business.

Not only that, they found time for one of the least predictable but most rewarding collaborations that folk music has produced, in the shape of two monumental albums, 20 years apart, with June Tabor. Much more about her later, but the potentially daunting task of singing along with the great diva of folk fell to the Oysters' front-man, John Jones, giving him the chance to prove again that he too is one of the great voices of the folk world.

Another thing about Jones; he was responsible for the folkiest tour ever, when he and his occasional band, the appropriately named Reluctant Ramblers, walked from venue to venue across the South of England! Never let it be said that this music lacks legs.

A Woman's Voice

IT was Maddy Prior who told me that Sandy Denny was dead.

Yes, yes, I know exactly how that reads. But let's be honest, there hasn't been much schmoozing with the folky and famous in this book so far. If you bump into someone you've been watching and listening to for a few decades, there might be a quick nod of recognition, a quiet 'How do' or 'How's it going?' but that's as far as it goes.

This was a bit of an exceptional situation, though. I knew, because it had been on the news that Sandy had fallen down a flight of stairs and, some days later, had collapsed at a friend's house and had been taken to hospital, but I didn't know how she was. Now here, in the same carriage as me on a train going to Blackpool, was her friend and fellow-folk princess, who would surely know. It wasn't surprising in itself that she should be there. Her father, the creator of *Z Cars*, Allan Prior, had worked, some years before my time, on the Blackpool evening paper and still lived there. So I took a deep breath, walked through the empty carriage, apologised for disturbing her and asked for a bulletin.

'She's dead,' she said, which was a bit of a conversation-stopper.

It was 1978, Denny was 31 and, in all honesty, not the least likely candidate for a premature and messy death. She had recently given birth to her daughter, Georgia, and that seemed to have intensified her problems with drugs and drink. Her friend, Linda Thompson, records her crashing her car with her baby in it and, on at least one occasion, forgetting her and leaving her in the pub, a feat only achieved since by David Cameron. Her husband, Trevor Lucas, no abstainer himself, became so alarmed by the situation that he took Georgia away to his native Australia.

She was in a coma for four days after being taken to hospital and died of what was described as a traumatic mid-brain haemorrhage. Her career was short but complicated - not a bad description of her as a person.

She can't have been easy to live with or work with, but, my oath, she could sing. She had already featured on a couple of albums, before briefly joining the Strawbs, years before their accidental hit record, 'Part of the Union.' When Fairport decided to get rid of their original singer, Judy Dyble, and held auditions, Sandy stood out 'like a clean glass in a sink full of dirty dishes,' according to silver-tongued founder-member Simon Nicol. Apart from her two stints with them, her reputation rests on her work with Fotheringay, the band she formed with Lucas - one LP at the time and another decades later - and a series of spell-binding solo albums. She appealed to both ends of her spectrum. She was voted best British female singer by what was essentially a rock readership at *Melody Maker*, but she was also the favourite singer of a folk academic like A.L. Lloyd. Bert, though, loses a brownie point with me for ungallantly referring to her as 'plump.' I would man the barricades over this. Plump? Never. Jean and Elaine Carruthers were plump; Sandy Denny was buxom, a word we get to use far too infrequently these days. I would also just about accept another, strictly northern adjective - bonny. I might have been biased; I realise now that she bore a strong resemblance to my girlfriend at the time - another short, complicated person. She couldn't sing, though.

I had a mate at Keele who was a hard-line, dogmatic fundamentalist on the subject of singers. He would only listen to women. 'Why on earth,' he used to ask, 'would you want to listen to a man singing when you could listen to a woman?' Denis was ten years older that the rest of us, most of it spent on the production-line at Wall's sausage factory. He was prematurely grey and held court sitting on his bed in his string-vest and Y-fronts, smoking his pipe and playing LPs by women singers. Naturally, he developed a bit of a reputation as a home-spun philosopher, but he had a complete block with the male voice. You might as well have told him to put on his best alpaca jacket and go on the pull in his hometown of Hyde, but for a man rather than a woman. It simply wouldn't have occurred to him.

Denis had a lot of Joan Baez - never guilty of singing like a man - but I was never all that keen. Too operatic for me by half, especially in her early days, before her voice got knocked about a bit. There are certain tracks now which do it for me - 'Diamonds and Rust,' 'The Night they Drove Old Dixie Down' or, from her vast Bob Dylan song-book, 'Farewell, Angelina' - but as a spotty adolescent I preferred Julie Felix as my Mexican-American songstress of choice. She was a bit of a cut-price alternative, but there was something more accessible and lived in about her voice.

I was also pretty struck with Judy Collins - the American singer, not to be confused with Shirley. She was essentially an interpreter of other people's songs, although she was not averse to raiding the tradition for something from left-field. A duet with a whale, for instance, on 'Farewell to Tarwathie,' a song which she presumably got from Bert Lloyd's *Leviathan*. She always had a great ear for an exceptional song, old or new, and when she heard 'Who Knows Where the Time Goes?' by an unknown English girl, Sandy Denny, she not only recorded it but made it the title track on her next album. It's a highly-polished rendition, but nobody has ever been able to sing it as well as its author. It's a remarkable piece of work, all the more so for being written when Denny was barely out of her teens. She wrote plenty of other memorable songs during her truncated life - not to mention singing some sensational versions of traditional songs - but nothing that summed her up, in all her vibrancy and melancholy, like 'Who Knows.....?'

The last time I saw her was at the Students' Union, just her and a piano. She sang 'Who Knows Where the Time Goes?' She sang 'Banks of the Nile,' perhaps her definitive treatment of a traditional song. She didn't have a huge voice; she couldn't belt it out above a hubbub like a man, like Janis Joplin, or even like a bigger-lunged folkie such as Maddy Prior. She was entirely dependent on being able to silence and seduce an audience - and an audience of half-pissed students at that. She had us hypnotised. 'That,' said Denis, 'is a woman's voice.'

Many years later, Oysterband wrote a song called 'Over the Water,' which has something to say about this chemistry. It is no co-incidence that many cultures have an equivalent of the Sirens, luring sailors to their doom with a song that is both intoxicating and dangerous. The Oysters simply sing: 'Two wild-eyed girls stood up among us ..... Held us silent with a song' and you know exactly what they mean. For me, it has usually been one wild-eyed girl at a time, but who's counting? Actually, the folk process has already been at work here. In the lyric insert, it says 'a wide-eyed girl,' but John Jones definitely sings 'two wild-eyed girls' and I prefer that version.

The first wild-eyed girl who held me silent was probably Marie Little, who, despite her name, was pretty big in the folk clubs in the 1960s. The one who would have rendered me speechless, probably for good, had I been one of the relatively small number of people who saw her sing in her prime, was Anne Briggs. When it comes to the wild-eyed index, she is right at the top, off the graph even. Her life, were she in a society that values what she does, would be the stuff not of one film, but of several. As a schoolgirl, she and a friend, cycled from their homes in Nottingham to Edinburgh to visit the singer, Archie Fisher. (That's one movie.) Still in her teens, Ewan MacColl heard her sing when he was taking a tour around the country, invited her to sing that night and added her to the tour. (There's another.) She became an item with Bert Jansch, living with him in a squat in London and teaching him 'Blackwaterside.' They looked so similar that most people took them for brother and sister. (And there's a blockbuster, 'Bert and Anne,' the folk world's answer to *Sid and Nancy*.) Subsequent relationships included a psychotic Scotsman who used to beat her up regularly and Johnny Moynihan, the bouzouki pioneer with whom she travelled the country, playing the occasional gig, in a horse-drawn caravan. (Possible TV sit-com.)

I say occasional, because she had a well-earned reputation for being too pissed and not turning up. Supposedly, she turned up to only five gigs between mid-

1963 and early-1965, because she was crippled by shyness and stage nerves. If you did see her, you were one of a privileged minority. I remember going to more than one concert for which she was on the bill, but she never showed. She did run into the sea in Donegal, though, to sing to the seals.

Under Moynihan's influence, she wrote her own songs and accompanied herself on bouzouki, but her real legacy is something far more primal. What she held MacColl and company silent with was her unaccompanied singing of traditional songs. Given that she hated the recording studio even more than the concert stage, it's a stroke of dumb luck that we have those early performances on CD. When her Topic recordings were re-released in 1990, her daughter had no inkling that she had ever been a singer. If you could have pinned her down in the 60s, she must have been extraordinary live - and it didn't hurt that she was very young and exotically beautiful, in a wild-eyed, Nottinghamshire sort of way. She is also unique in the folk world in having her life chronicled by other singers. Sandy Denny's 'The Pond and the Stream' is about her; so is Richard Thompson's 'Beeswing.'

So you see why I was excited to see that, after two decades of silence, she was on the bill at Farnham Folk Day, which was serendipitously scheduled for the day after the Challenge Cup final at Wembley.

Anne Briggs' long-awaited comeback was in a side-room at the arts centre, with maybe a hundred crammed in. If I was pitching this to Hollywood, it would be a triumphant happy ending, possibly with Meryl Streep in the lead role. What happened in reality was this. A pale, drawn, middle-aged woman in jeans stood up, looked embarrassed and started, amid the deepest silence I've ever experienced at a gig, to sing. The voice was still there; a little worn around the edges, but then it would be. She still had a wonderful way with a lyric; an instinct for what to embellish and what to leave well alone. When people tell me that Whitney Houston or Celine Dion are great singers, I think 'Very clever.... but far too many notes.' With Anne Briggs, it seems to me, there's so much going on within the notes that you don't need as many of them.

She sang three songs; I couldn't even tell you what they were, other than fantastic. Mid-way through the fourth, she simply froze, couldn't make another sound and fled. As far as I know, she has not sung in public since.

She is not the only woman to have lost her voice for a decade or two. It happened to Linda Thompson, Richard's ex. Shirley Collins doesn't sing any more. It's what Leonard Cohen - ironically in his case - calls 'the gift of a golden voice' and, in the nature of a gift, it can be snatched back at any time. Fortunately, there are many, many more who have held me silent, rather than falling silent themselves. Pride of place has to go to June Tabor, the grande dame of folk-song. Since the early 70s, she has been the classiest of class acts. She treats folk music as High Art, very much with the capital letters, which might not be the only way to approach it, but it is certainly one way. When she was a librarian in Haringey, she used to go to work on the same train as my mate, Dave, he of Gerald and the Geraniums. Under the flimsy pretext of going into his school to help out with some rugby league coaching, I caught that train. In reality, it was to check out whether it was genuinely the same person. I know, it's on the border-line of stalking, but they didn't have a name for it back then.

June got the bug by hearing traditional songs for the first time on the television God-slot show, *Hallelujah!* Her older sister bought a copy of Anne Briggs' EP, *The Hazards of Love*, and she slowed it down to 33 rpm and copied it, note for note and nuance for nuance. 'I was captivated by this woman's voice and what she did with it,' she says in the notes for her boxed set, *Always*. All her records begin with the letter A, by the way, which I can only believe is some sort of fiendishly cunning librarian's plan to by-pass the alphabetical cataloguing system.

Gradually, her own style evolved, at the same time as she was studying Modern and Medieval Languages at Oxford. Once heard, you would not confuse her with anyone else. For one thing, she sings in a lower register than any comparable female vocalist. For another, she has a particular way of decorating a note with what her sometime collaborator, Andrew Cronshaw, describes as a 'shiver' of her jaw. It works for the unaccompanied traditional songs with which she started; it also works for the contemporary material of which she has become the prime interpreter - songs like Eric Bogle's 'The Band Played Waltzing Matilda' - a hit in Ireland for the Clancy Brothers, incidentally - and any number by Richard Thompson. Whatever she sings, she brings a certain gravitas to it. There is a hint of the Joan Bakewells about her; the thinking man's Siren?

I've heard people say that, magnificent though she is, a full evening spent in June's company can be a slightly chilly experience. I don't agree, but I know where they are coming from. She has a well-earned reputation for singing very dark songs. There are a lot of deaths and broken hearts in a June Tabor concert - and a certain rigour and seriousness. She can seem austere and even a tad severe in her black stage clothes. You aren't really encouraged to join in the choruses, any more than the Berlin Philharmonic would want you to bring along your kazoo and play along with the catchy bits. She used to run a restaurant in Cumbria and I'll have a bet that there weren't many frivolous complaints about the food.

For all that, she can be very funny, in a droll, deadpan sort of way. It's no coincidence that she is the best-known performer of the knockabout folk-song parodies of Les Barker. She has also proved wonderfully adaptable to working with others and in other styles. She has made an album of jazz standards and sung in French and German. There were two albums with Maddy Prior - very much her mentor in the early years - and two, 20 years apart, with Oysterband. That latter collaboration showed a different aspect of her talents, working with a full-on rock backing and having a whale of a time. The live dates they did were unforgettable, but I would go to see her Anyway, Anytime, Anywhere - to stick to her favourite end of the alphabet.

One gig - although that seems too careless and casual a word for it - that sticks in the mind was at the Holywell Music Room in Oxford, an atmospheric old building, claimed to be the oldest concert hall in Europe, where she particularly loves to sing. It was sold out and I had no ticket, but I would always back myself to blag my way in under those circumstances. Martin Carthy says that, from an itinerant performer's point of view, the worse the journey the better the gig. There is another unwritten rule of folk; the further you have travelled, the more moral right you have to get in, ticket or no ticket.

'But I've come all the way from Bolton,' I sob-storied them on the door. 'Specially.'

It wasn't quite true. I was in Oxford to check out whether the university would be good enough for my literary middle daughter. Perhaps she should study French and Latin at St Hugh's and appear on *University Challenge* like June? Anyway, I was convincing enough for them to let me in to perch on the edge of a pew somewhere - and it was the most intense I've ever seen her.

I would have loved, however, to have been at the same venue on another occasion, which she describes on *Always*. She got to the end of her set and, for her inevitable encore, planned to sing 'Waiting for the Lark' by Bill Caddick - a particularly poignant and melancholy piece. Only one problem; she couldn't remember the words of the first verse. Nor could any of her musicians; nor could anyone in the audience. Then came inspiration. Had anyone bought the CD it was on at half-time? Yes, one hand went up, and everyone waited while he painstakingly removed the cellophane, extracted the lyric sheet and read out the elusive words. What larks, indeed. But don't anyone try to tell me that June Tabor doesn't have a lighter side.

'Sleep on child, it is almost day.....' it goes, by the way. Had I been there, I could have told them that.

If there is a potential inheritor of the crown as First Voice of Folk, not that Ms Tabor is planning to abdicate, it is probably Eliza Carthy, and she could hardly be more different. Eliza would also complicate things by insisting that she is not even the best female singer in her family, not while her mum, Norma Waterson, is around. We last encountered Norma during the heyday of the Watersons as the group that re-defined unaccompanied singing, until she went off to be a DJ in the West Indies. On her return, she remained a Waterson, but also became a Carthy by marrying Martin, who in turn became a Waterson. With the addition of Eliza, the product of this quite unfair collision of genes, they became Waterson:Carthy. Norma, however, merits attention as a solo performer and distinctive voice in her own right. Hers is the classic example of one that has improved with age.

It was never a pretty-pretty voice, but it could carry a

song like few others. As time has gone on, it has acquired the fine lines of experience, whilst her phrasing is an object lesson for younger singers. She is equally at home with her vast store of traditional song or the contemporary material that made up an album that was nominated for the Mercury Music Prize. I remember Tony Parsons reviewing it on BBC2 and admitting that he could not cope with the 'Englishness' of her voice. That is a little glimpse of insight into the cultural dislocation of mainstream taste; there is nothing as forbiddingly exotic as the hidden roots buried in your own garden.

Nor should we neglect Norma's late sister, Elaine Waterson - always known as Lal. A fine singer herself, although often the second voice when singing with Norma, she will probably be remembered most of all for the haunting quality of her own songs. June Tabor calls them 'cinematic' in the way they conjure up a series of images that add up not necessarily to a narrative, but to a mood. They are strange, beautifully brittle things, although she did have her exuberant moments, as in the joyous 'Some Old Salty,' a maritime song Eliza has been able to introduce on stage as 'a shanty from my auntie.'

Eliza has been able to build upon the foundations laid down by her family, to celebrate their achievements without being cowed by them. It was daunting to realise recently that she, the baby of the household, was also celebrating 21 years as a professional musician. She has done it her way, with a dash of punk attitude to toughen up the folk festival chic.

June Tabor says that the driving force behind her own music has always been the lyrics; Eliza's has been driven by the fiddle that she plays with such power and passion. That is where it all begins, but her singing commands equal attention. It falls into two areas, which do not generally intersect with each other. The first is her bold approach to breathing new energy into English traditional songs and tunes; the second consists of her own, often quirky compositions, which have accounted for three albums on their own. It is already a formidable body of work, although it was interrupted by a polyp on her vocal chords that effectively silenced her for a year or more. It was a huge relief, therefore, to her legions of fans to find her restored to full vocal vigour on her 21st anniversary tour. I saw her in Saltaire, near Bradford, with an 11-piece band, and she has never sounded as good.

If there is another young woman coming at it from approximately the same direction, it would have to be Bella Hardy. She sings, she writes, she plays the fiddle. She gets a bonus point from me for coming from Edale in Derbyshire and another for writing a song as perfect as 'Three Black Feathers' when she was still studying for her A-levels. For sheer precocity, that beats even Sandy Denny's 'Who Knows Where the Time Goes?'

Sometimes you hear a singer with whom you think you are going to have a long-term relationship, but for some reason it doesn't work out. It was like that with Cara Dillon. The first time I heard her, I thought it was the real thing, but I tired of her. It makes me feel a little like the heartless lothario in Eliza Carthy's 'Little Big Man': 'He likes them once, then he don't like them any more.'

If it's Irish songstresses you're after, there's more depth to my mind in Niamh Parsons, Susan McKeown or my all-time Irish favourite, Dolores Keane. I once saw her at a near-deserted town hall in either Nelson or Colne - never been quite sure which was which - and her voice filled the place.

Then there's the Kate Rusby question. Now, Kate

seems a lovely lass and has done more than most to bring this music to the masses. But when she was in a duo with Kathryn Roberts - I made a mad dash to Newcastle-under-Lyme, of all places, to see their last gig together - it was the other voice that grabbed me and still does.

This takes us back into the murky waters of more than one woman singing at the same time, which almost qualifies as cheating. Twin Sirens; multiple Sirens even. What's a boy to do? Lash himself to the main-mast? Particularly adept at this form of sorcery were the wittily-named Witches of Elswick. They were four unaccompanied women singers. (By which I don't mean that they turned up at gigs on their own. Nor is it true that, in certain Arabic countries, female singers have to be accompanied by a male relative.) Their four-part harmonies were head-spinning and when they went their separate ways, one of them turned out to be Fay Hield, another candidate for the title of the finest woman singer of her generation. She was the first new artist to be signed by the prestigious Topic label for a decade. That might be a slightly depressing statistic, but her singing of unfamiliar songs in unfamiliar ways makes her a suitable exception to the rule. She is also a key figure later in this story.

For female duos, family ties seem to be a major factor; or they do in the case of two pairs of sisters who have given me goose-bumps - and not just by leaving a window open. I was first directed to the McGarrigles by a flat-mate who flourished their first LP and said: 'Isn't that the girl you've been going out with?' Sure enough, Anna McGarrigle was the spitting image of the woman who was to become, several tangled years later, Mrs Wrong Notes.

Despite their surname, Kate and Anna were French-Canadian. Individually, they sounded great, in French or English. Put them together in any language and they were devastating, but one thing they were not burdened with was a lot of stage-craft. I first saw them at the Free Trade Hall and there was something girlishly shambolic about them as they prattled and giggled between numbers; then they would sing and it all made sense. Scroll forward 20 years and here they are again, but now more like a pair of slightly batty aunts, muttering at each other, affectionately chivvying and bickering. Then they launch into something from that first album - either 'Mendocino' or 'Heart Like a Wheel' - and I find that, quite unexpectedly, there are tears running down my cheeks. I'm there with my eldest daughter and I have a crafty side-long glance to make sure that she hasn't seen this deplorably un-English display of emotion - and she is in floods of tears as well. It's all in the genes, you see. Our family might not be able to sing in harmony, but, by god, we can blub in unison.

Kate died in 2010, better known by this stage as the mother of Rufus and Martha Wainwright. The good news is that Mrs Wrong Notes still looks like a young Anna McGarrigle - or she does to me, at any rate.

Their successors in the heartbreak harmony business, for my money, are the Unthanks. They are two sisters from the North East, the elder of them, Rachel, is a fine singer. The rest of the band all do their bit admirably, but the really unique instrument they have at their disposal is the voice of Becky Unthank. I've never heard anything remotely like it. It's pitched somewhere up in the stratosphere; down at ground level, it's as much a breath as it is a sound.

The other great things about the Unthanks are their energy and innovation. Not content with merely doing what they know they can do, they have stretched their wings with a series of what they call *Diversions*. One was a show and an album devoted to the songs of Robert Wyatt and Antony and the Johnsons - strange territory for much of their fan-base, I suspect. Another side-project was a film and soundtrack about the ship-building industry. Best of all was their collaboration with the Brighouse and Rastrick Brass Band, bringing together two musical worlds that live alongside each other but rarely overlap. From the first note, it works triumphantly. It happens to be a song about a racing pigeon called 'The King of Rome,' written by a man in Derby named Dick Cadbury and first popularised by June Tabor. My mate Keith, surely my most successful convert to folk music, is perhaps an even bigger Unthanks fan than I am. He took his girlfriend, Julie, to see them with the Brighouse and Rastrick. Halfway through the first song, she looked in his direction and there were tears trickling down his face. 'Keith,' she said, rather severely, 'it's about a bloody pigeon.'

Ah yes, but not just any pigeon. This one is in a glass case in Derby Museum. It wouldn't surprise me if, on one of their days out, they call in to see it. On their ship-building tour, we saw The Unthanks in Preston, at a pub with long, communal tables for pre-gig nosh. We thus found ourselves sharing with Rachel and her baby, helping out as best we could with the feeding and the changing. You don't get to do that with Beyonce.

I ticked one of my empty boxes recently, when I saw Julie Murphy with her band Fernhill. I'd always loved her singing, solo or with the group. Among other things, she sings my all-time favourite version of 'Polly Vaughan,' the strange old ballad about the young man who shoots and kills his lover when he mistakes her for a swan. A rather unlikely line of defence, you think, but then along bounds Oscar Pistorius. The folk have always had over-active imaginations, but sometimes even they struggle to keep up with what purports to be contemporary reality.

The closest I'd come to seeing her in person was in Oxford, the night after June Tabor. It was also sold out, but I thought that pulling the 'All the way from Bolton' scam two nights running was a bit much. Ms Murphy would not be everyone's cup of tea; for one thing, she sings mainly in Welsh, although she is not Welsh herself. It didn't bother me and that set me thinking about how important or otherwise the meaning is when you're seduced by a voice or voices.

Not very, when Márta Sebestyén is singing in Hungarian, or for the massed voices of the Le Mystère des Voix Bulgares or the Mahotela Queens from South Africa, or anything in Gaelic, of course. Perhaps there is something about hearing women sing in a language you don't understand that echoes ordinary life.

Perhaps too, Denis had a point when he argued that life was just too short to spend any of it listening to anything without a woman's voice in it.

A little cameo in conclusion then, which seems to support his thesis. At a gig by Jon Boden's occasional band, the Remnant Kings, the plan was that after the concert proper, there would be an informal singaround in the bar. Not surprisingly, it's the hairy-chested end of the repertoire that tends to dominate at these occasions; bearded men with pints singing shanties like 'General Taylor' and 'Stormalong.' In the middle of this, a blonde wisp of a girl is persuaded to sing. 'I don't know many sea-shanties,' she admits and sings a quiet, slow version of a song called 'Icarus' - Greek chap. Flies too near the sun. You already know the ending.

But we all fell silent to hear it again and make sure that, just for once, he didn't fly home in triumph, like the King of Rome, long after everyone had given him up for lost.

Laughter in the Dark: Richard Thompson and Leonard Cohen

FOLK music is inevitably and irredeemably miserable. That's one thing everybody knows about it, along with the beards and the fingers in the ears.

Performers gleefully collude with this image, asking audiences: 'Do you want my one happy song or ten more mournful ones?' Admittedly, there is a lot of war, death and thwarted love in folk song, but you've not got to let it get you down.

I had a bad reputation in the house I shared in Blackpool for resorting, at times of deep despair, to wallowing in a track from *The Transports* called 'The Black and Bitter Night.' It was written by the future suicide, Peter Bellamy, and sung with maximum dolefulness by Mike Waterson, but it wasn't as optimistic as that makes it sound. It got a few extra spins when my mum died in her early 50s, finally worn down by her recurring bouts of cancer.

For all that, there are laughs to be had from the

supposedly black and bitter terrain. Apart from the massed ranks of folk club comedians, there are the hysterical parodies of Les Barker and the East Coast's answer to the Coppers - the Kipper Family. The professional comic, Ade Edmondson, has a band - the Bad Shepherds - who play old punk hits in traditional Irish style. It's basically one joke, but it's a good one, well executed, and my son, Sam, enjoys it as much as his other folk favourites, Lau. Even June Tabor, for heaven's sake, plays it for laughs on occasion.

Nevertheless, the myth stubbornly persists that folk takes itself too seriously. It would be closer to the truth to say that we are quite willing to take the piss out of ourselves, but we don't like anyone else doing it. A good example of doing it to ourselves was the title of a bootleg Richard Thompson cassette - yes, we are going back a bit - entitled *Doom and Gloom from the Tomb: Volume One*. I particularly like the deadpan 'Volume One', as though it is inevitable that there will be more Doom and Gloom to follow. There is actually a Volume Two, entitled *Over my Dead Body*, but I've never tracked down a copy.

Thompson is the high priest of the misery-guts tendency in British folk music, or he is popularly supposed to be. In fact, it seems to me that it is a reputation he enjoys and encourages because it provides him with endless amusement.

There are tragic elements in his story. His girlfriend, Jeannie Franklyn, died in Fairport Convention's motorway crash. His first marriage disintegrated in public, on stage during an American tour. It must have been horrible for both of them, but the tension in the air produced some of the most visceral music a man and a woman can make on stage. He got religion, but retained his humanity.

That last life-changing event introduces an immediate

paradox. He has spent most of his life as a Sufi Muslim and yet no-one writes more vividly about the pleasures and pains of getting blind drunk, from 'Down Where the Drunkards Roll' onwards. He used to enjoy it himself, but it's an awfully long time for it to survive as a recurring theme of his work. Likewise, the longer he spends in Santa Monica, the stronger the influence of his upbringing in the suburbs of North London on his writing. Sometimes, he winds back a whole generation, to an imagined Scottish borderland from which his father came. It all adds to the layered complexity of what he does - and what makes him such a rewarding artist to follow.

It was his precocious guitar work with Fairport that first marked him out as something special - and still would, even if he had never written or sung a note. The range of guitarists who acknowledge him as a major influence - on acoustic or electric - includes the likes of Johnny Marr and Mark Knopfler and qualifies him as that rare bird, a musician's musician.

Almost as precocious was his skill as a composer. 'Meet on the Ledge,' for instance, was written when he was 19, but already mining the seams of nostalgia and regret over times lost. He wrote some memorable songs for Fairport in tandem with Dave Swarbrick, but left the band because he wanted to concentrate on his own material. That raised the question of who was going to sing it, because that had been the slowest of his abilities to develop. Perhaps because of the vestiges of a childhood stammer, he largely avoided singing with Fairport. On his first solo album, *Henry the Human Fly,* he didn't so much avoid it as apologise for it, with his vocals so far back in the mix that they are effectively camouflaged. His musical partnership with his first wife, Linda Peters, solved that problem. By the time of their messy split, he had become a confident singer.

But a singer of what? Manifestos of misery and hopelessness? Well, yes, but it has been more fun than that.

Admittedly, Richard Thompson is very good at bleak; at dark, pessimistic songs like 'End of the Rainbow' and 'The Great Valerio.' The surprise to anyone coming afresh to his work, but aware of his reputation, is how cheery he can be.

One of his early songs even has the word 'jolly' in its title; okay, it also has the word 'hangman,' but you get the idea. The subject matter of a Thompson concert might look a tad depressing, but you invariably come out on a high, or I always have - and I've seen him perform too many times to count.

Here, however, is a virtual RT gig designed to rehabilitate him among those who like their music happy. Depressing, my hat. You should be able to get it on the National Health.

RICHARD THOMPSON'S 20 HAPPIEST SONGS

(*In approximate chronological order*)

MEET ON THE LEDGE

Nostalgia and regret, certainly, but at the end of the day an optimistic anthem. 'If you really mean it, it all comes round again.'

NOBODY'S WEDDING

The biggest rib-tickler on *Henry the Human Fly*, complete with out-of-tune accordion coda.

I WANT TO SEE THE BRIGHT LIGHTS TONIGHT

How did this not turn out to be his accidental hit, in either the original by him and Linda, or the cover by the then-bankable Julie Covington? It has all the right ingredients:

catchiness, a euphoric, up-for-the-weekend afirmation of life - and the CWS Silver Band! Ah, what might have been.

WHEN I GET TO THE BORDER
Patrick Humphries, in his RT biography, *Strange Affair*, says that 'Bright Lights' is the only upbeat track on the album of the same name. What about this one? Okay, things aren't too great, but there's an escape route, a border to cross.

SMIFFY'S GLASS EYE
On some solo tours, Richard Thompson has set himself the considerable challenge of doing requests from his back catalogue shouted out by the audience. The night I was there, someone called out for 'Smiffy's Glass Eye,' an obscure song from the forgettable album, *Hokey Pokey*. He peered suspiciously into the stalls and asked: 'Were you in Harpenden last night?' I love the idea of this geezer following him around the country crying out in vain for 'Smiffy's Glass Eye.' Another highlight from that gig; an old mate gave me his front-row seat when he had to leave at half-time to pick up his son from ice-hockey training.

HOKEY POKEY
Forgettable album, but there's no denying the jollity of this paean to ice cream and back-street sex.

NEW ST GEORGE
A rallying cry for a new sort of patriotism. The essential message is that things can get better if we all get together for a cèilidh.

TIME TO RING SOME CHANGES
See above.

WALL OF DEATH
Despite the D-word in the title, this is a cleverly disguised celebration of life and risk-taking. 'You can waste your time on the other rides ..... This is the nearest to being alive.'

HOW MANY TIMES?
Not many, if you're looking for recorded versions of this rollicking mandolin tune.

TEAR-STAINED LETTER
Again, don't be fooled by the title, because this is a rip-roaring rocker guaranteed to cheer you up; especially a 20-minute version with a horn section in overdrive, on a Friday night at Cropredy.

1952 VINCENT BLACK LIGHTNING
A Thompson classic; part Bonnie and Clyde, part border ballad, part black and white cops and robbers B-movie from Elstree Studios. The owner of the motorbike winds up dying of shot-gun wounds, but in a very triumphant and uplifting way.

FEEL SO GOOD
Another audience favourite. Alright, the protagonist is a psycho, fresh out of jail and high as a kite on pills and testosterone, but he knows how to have a good time.

DON'T SIT ON MY JIMMY SHANDS
Worth including for its title alone. A plaintive plea for care that will strike a chord with anyone who has ever taken unpopular music to a party. Plenty of us could re-write it as 'Don't Sit on my Richard Thompsons.'

VALERIE
Always a show-stopper, not least for some of the most exuberant bad rhymes ever manufactured. "I can't afford her on my salary ...... But I wait, wait, wait for Valerie.'

MGB GT
Love song to a sports car, unaccountably never used in their advertising. But then neither was 'Vincent Black Lightning.' Come to think of it, both firms were probably long out of business before the songs saw the light of day.

TURNING OF THE TIDE
A jaunty little number about getting old and dying.

JOHNNY'S FAR AWAY
A modern couple survive separation by the rolling sea. Notable for its juxtaposition of 'Bahamas' and 'pyjamas'.

BAD MONKEY
More valuable relationship advice from the acknowledged expert.

TWO LEFT FEET
Bad dancing and audience participation compulsory.

ENCORE: CRASH THE PARTY
Does what it says on the label. The party must be carrying on somewhere.

And there you are, the most uplifting musical evening you could ever have, even without resorting to sure-fire winners like the scurrilous 'Dear Janet Jackson' or the Britney Spears hit, 'Oops!... I did it Again,' one of many highlights from his show, *1,000 Years of Popular Music*. It even leaves out one of his own favourite encore numbers, The Who's 'Substitute.' It also ignores the wealth of throw-away comic lines in otherwise serious songs. There was once talk of a full CD of Richard Thompson's humorous songs, but it was eventually decided that it would have been just too much hilarity. It is all what my grandchildren would call 'too much fun.' Unless, of course, you are intent on an unbroken diet of doom and gloom, a two-hour version of 'Calvary Cross,' perhaps; but for that you have come to the wrong man.

The trick is to separate the singer from the song. People want it all to be autobiographical, but, as far as Thompson is concerned, he is playing a series of roles. Sometimes the persona adopted is that of an introspective nerd, sometimes that of a volcano waiting to erupt, as in 'Feel so Good.' As he says in Humphries' *Strange Affair*: 'I don't think of the songs as being gloomy. I think of them as being serious, about serious subjects. Most of them are, in fact, optimistic ..... Shakespeare wrote a lot of tragedies, but you don't go and stick your head in the gas oven because you've seen *Hamlet*.'

In *RT: The Life and Music of Richard Thompson*, he reveals that the first record he ever bought was 'A Four-legged Friend' by Roy Rogers and Trigger. He says that the B-side, 'There's a Cloud in my Valley of Sunshine,' has influenced his song-writing from that day on, but that, of course, is a typically sardonic, self-deprecating Thompson joke.

I have met Richard Thompson just the once, if you can call it a meeting at all. By some weird co-incidence, we were both looking in the window of the same estate agents in the Cotswolds - it must have been a side-trip from Cropredy - marvelling at the prices and agreeing that neither of us could afford anything around there.

I've searched his songs since for any oblique reference to this conversation, but nothing so far. The point is that, whilst it is no surprise or injustice that I cannot run to a cottage in the Cotswolds, he should, if there was any fairness in life, have the wherewithal for a full street of the honey-coloured stone houses in somewhere like Chipping Norton.

I've no doubt that he lives well enough in California and London, but his record sales have never made him rich and probably now never will. Songs and albums that are adored by his fans have completely by-passed a wider audience. Warner Brothers, who released *Henry the Human Fly* in America, once said that it was the worst-selling record they had ever had. Elvis Costello has described him as Britain's greatest-ever singer-songwriter, but Richard's sales are a fraction of those of Mr McManus. He can fill venues on either side of the Atlantic, but he remains that endangered species, the cult hero.

Why does he still rank as British music's best-kept secret? Is it the reputation for misery? The business ineptitude with which various phases of his career have been conducted? His own estimate that three-quarters of his audience are men? There's something in this. The guitar virtuosity is of far more interest to blokes, but Thompson himself thinks that his songs are at least as woman-friendly as they are male orientated. That's not quite my experience. Every girlfriend I ever had and every female family member since have heard plenty of Richard Thompson. They have all said the same thing: Alright in small doses. A bit depressing after that.

Even Patrick Humphries has provided fuel for their fire, describing early Thompson as 'making Leonard Cohen sound like Barry Manilow.'

Talking of which.....

I NEVER cared much for Laughing Leonard Cohen. Fair enough, I could appreciate the poetic integrity of the songs, but the mode of his delivery did nothing for me at all. It had to do with the unexpressive voice, the rather prissy guitar style. There was also an issue of over-familiarity.

Leonard Cohen albums were just about compulsory in the early 70s; I was one of the very few people I knew who didn't have one - apart from those who wouldn't listen to male singers on principle. I joined forces with that tendency by preferring Judy Collins' version of 'Suzanne,' which was close to heresy in student bed-sit land.

In years to come, he vanished off my radar completely, except as a short-hand for a particular sort of navel-gazing and philosophical pretension which I instinctively disliked. Or thought I did.

Then I had my Road to Montreal moment, one I can only describe, given the way Cohen dealt almost exclusively in religious imagery, as an epiphany. It happened in a very strange way, on a working trip to Carcassonne in the South of France. A gang of us went out for a meal, probably the local speciality of cassoulet. It came with a side-dish of green beans in garlic, but it would be more accurate to describe that as a bowl of garlic with the occasional green bean afloat in it. It was irresistible. Now, it seems that one of the lesser-known properties of garlic, apart from repelling vampires and rendering elephant-leg kebabs edible, is that, in industrial quantities, it can induce insomnia. That was certainly the effect it had on me that night in Le Grand Hôtel Terminus. After several sleepless hours, I turned on the TV and hoped that it could rock me off. It was a late-night music video show - very late night, by this time - and, in among the Johnny Hallyday and Petula Clark, or whatever the French were listening to at the time, the first song that tweaked my interest was one called 'Closing Time,' a sort of warped hoe-down, a dystopian line-dance. It was filmed in black and white and, in the middle of all the mayhem and the woozy expanses of female flesh, there was a face I recognised.

'I know him,' I said with all the shock of spotting your granny in a brothel. 'That's miserable old Leonard Cohen.' I had plenty of chance to study the finer points, because it was repeated every half-hour; someone at the Carcassonne TV station had got the Cohens real bad. By the morning, I had it engrained in my mind and it has been there ever since. In some ways, it's the least representative Cohen track you could find; he doesn't play a lot of barn-dances.

Apparently, the video was filmed at the Rodeo Club, a country and western venue in Toronto. It won an award, a Canadian Grammy no less, and it was pretty big in Carcassonne as well. All the way home I was humming and singing in the most infuriating manner:

> 'So we're drinking and we're dancing
> And the band is really happening
> And the Johnny Walker wisdom running high
> And my very sweet companion
> She's the Angel of Compassion
> And she's rubbing half the world against her
> thigh.'

You get the picture. I went straight out and bought a copy of the album it's on - *The Future* - and drove everyone mad with it at home. In fact, somewhere along the line, I've acquired two. It wouldn't surprise me if I got home one night and found that there were three. I went forward and backwards into his other albums; it just wasn't the lugubrious Leonard I remembered. His voice was somewhere between a growl and a whisper; it no longer sounded like the posturing of a young man, but like the genuine and hard-won experience of an old man - he was 58 when *The Future* came out. Old, yes, but not as we know it. His biographer, Anthony Reynolds, records in *Leonard Cohen: A Remarkable Life* what he said whilst promoting that album.

'This idea that your creative impetus is over by 30, that you immolate yourself on this pyre of energy and sexuality and can then go back to cleaning up and doing the dishes ..... it just ain't so. The fire continues to burn fiercely as you get older.'

I'm inclined to take his word for it, or, as he said on his previous album, there 'Ain't No Cure For Love.' Cohen conducts himself as though you wouldn't want one. On and off stage, he dresses as formally and immaculately as a Mafia don at a funeral. On and off stage, he enjoys the company of women a fraction of his age. It's not what you associate with a Buddhist monk, which he also is. It's reassuring, really, that like Richard Thompson becoming a Muslim but retaining his irreverent wit, he can cut the mustard in the mustard-coloured robe, but remain a randy old goat. Part Dalai Lama, part Benny Hill.

Irony has a way of exacting a price for all that balancing on unmatched step-ladders. In 2005, Cohen discovered that Kelley Lynch, his manager and sometime lover, had been happily helping herself to his various bank accounts for years, to the extent that there was little left.

He didn't rant and rage. His most extreme quote from the time was that it was 'enough to put a dent in your mood.' Despite his popular image, he didn't wallow in self-pity. Instead, at the age of 71, he went back on the road, and for that, ironically, we have Kelley Lynch to thank. And thank her we should, because his work since he entered his eighth decade has been the most remarkable of his life. Far more than callow youths like Dylan and Jagger, both ten years younger, he has become what they were once called - The Spokesman for a Generation. The generation in question is the romantically inclined over-60s, 70s or 80s, depending on just where you stand on that pathway.

I missed the chance to see him on his 2008 tour, the one that produced the epic *Live in London* double CD. The ticket prices were such that they invited you to share in his financial distress. He apologised to the audience for being away since his mid-60s - 'Just a kid with a crazy dream,' he said. More remarkably, his biographer has never seen him perform either. The closest he has come was in Spain, where Cohen collapsed with food poisoning and everyone assumed he had died on stage. Not a bit of it, he was back in action the following night, but Reynolds had moved on. You could take that as a metaphor for the elusiveness of his subject.

All the Wrong Steps: A Brief Digression into the Arcane World of Folk Dance

FOLK song enthusiasts and folk dance people loathe each other. It's another of those things that everybody knows and, surprisingly, there is a germ of truth in it.

I blame the EFDSS - the English Folk Dance and Song Society - or rather I blame it for provocatively placing the D in front of the first S, for prioritising dance ahead of song. If it had been the EFSDS, that would have been fine, although it could have triggered a *Life of Brian* style proliferation of warring factions. The Folk Song and Dance Society of England (FSDSE) taking on the Society of Folk Dance and Song in England (Marxist-Leninist) and the rest.

I also blame that Cecil Sharp. The composer and collector founded the English Folk Dance Society in 1911 and it merged with the Folk Song Society in 1932. Ever since, the singers have complained about dancers cluttering up Cecil Sharp House in North London with their capering, whilst the dancers moaned about the bellowing from the basement.

If anything has a bigger image problem than English folk song, it is English folk dance. If anything is synonymous with the twee and the naff in the popular imagination, it is morris dancing. It doesn't have to be that way; it can be the English haka, to cite the New Zealand ceremonial dance that Kiwis break into at the slightest excuse.

By morris dancing, most people mean what they see outside pubs in summer, all white hankies and bells, although some have it mixed up with maypole dancing, which even I think is pretty twee. There is another strand of morris, though, which is all about clogs, clashing clubs and pent-up aggression. Watch a good Northern morris side lay into each other with their sticks and it's positively dangerous. It can also be pretty intimidating performed en masse. I once came out of the London Underground at Trafalgar Square to find it full of morris sides all dancing in unison for the biggest morris-fest ever seen. It was Rugby League Challenge Cup final weekend and half a dozen fully kitted-out St Helens supporters joined in, initially to take the mick, but then they found that they actually quite enjoyed it. In among the dozens of teams in their bell, breeches and bonnets, there was a little island of white shirts with a big red V. The closest thing I've seen to that mass morris was a festival on the square in front of the railway station in Huddersfield, with a score or more of teams taking their turns to dance.

One chap, resplendent in his kit - green velvet knee-breeches and doublet - went into the King's Head on the station for a refreshing pint. A couple of local lads were at the bar and one gave the other a nudge in the ribs. 'Nay lad, don't mess with them,' the second man says. 'I got in a fight with a morris dancer once. He knocked seven bells out of me.'

You certainly wouldn't want to mess with a group I saw at a Shrewsbury Festival, because Black Crow Morris are the stuff of nightmares. Forget the crisp white shirts and shiny shoes, the sunshine on the pub car-park. These boys dress more like survivors of Armageddon, with ripped and tattered black clothing and - more controversially - blacked-up faces. The term sinister does not begin to do them justice.

What they are is the militant wing of the border morris revival, a different tradition from the more familiar Cotswold style, and which used to thrive in the hills where Shropshire meets Wales. One of its characteristics is the black-face, which makes some people a little queasy in the 21st century. Theories abound as to its origins; one clue could lie in the very word 'morris,' which could be a corruption of 'Moorish' and imply North African roots. On the other hand, it could have something to do with the American minstrel shows, which, shooting off in another direction led to the insanely popular *Black and White Minstrel Show*, a staple of weekend television when there were only two or three channels. Or, if you prefer it, you can subscribe to the explanation that the burnt cork is essentially a disguise, supposed to protect the identity of the dancers when their tradition was considered seditious or irreligious. What we do know about this school of morris is that there is something of the night about it, something pagan and vaguely threatening. Danced regularly at state occasions, it would improve them no end.

Part of the appeal of the morris to the tiny proportion of the population who do not feel that it is a condition of their birthright that they sneer at it, is the music that goes along with it. It can be as basic as a drum and whistle, or as turbo-charged as the great folk-rock albums issued under the *Morris On* banner. Since the original in 1971, there has been *Son of Morris On* and *Grandson of Morris On* and *Great Grandson of Morris On*. Now we're onto *The Mother of All Morris* and I'm not quite sure where we go from there. The electrification of morris dance tunes has become a little cottage industry, although folk dance people sometimes complain that they are played too fast. Too fast or too slow, the great contribution the tunes make to the survival of the morris is that musicians love to play them. They are addictive and you get the impression that even musicians with a wide spectrum of activities would be quite happy if you told them that in future they could only play morris tunes.

My own relationship with dance has always been tangential. If I had two left hands, I could equally claim three left feet. The dancing was always something vaguely enjoyable going on around the fringes of the music. In the early 70s at Keele, when the hippies were wandering around the campus naked, we had a rapper team. This was before the term 'rapper' denoted a dude with too much jewellery intoning about his hoes and his hood. Back then, it meant a family of dances, usually from Yorkshire or the North-East, involving a complicated manipulation of 'swords' - not real ones, that would be taking the human sacrifice overtones a little too far. They can be quite gymnastic affairs, with members of teams performing somersaults worthy of Premier League footballers.

Dance plays a role in a number of groups' stage acts. No Unthanks gig is complete without Becky donning the clogs and Maddy Prior's fancy footwork is recognised in the song 'When Maddy Dances.' It is the Irish, however, who have taken the folk-dance of the British Isles onto a world stage. It is a style all of its own, with the feet and legs working a frenzied overtime whilst the arms and trunk remain uncannily motionless. It is, even by the standards of folk dancing, an easy one to take the Michael Flatleys out of; and yet it has produced the global phenomenon that is *Riverdance.*

It started life as the half-time entertainment when Ireland hosted the Eurovision Song Contest and people just took to the idea of choreographed jig and reels. Oddly enough, the ringmaster that night, Terry Wogan, also had a folk-dance hit with 'The Floral Dance'.

I've never seen the Cornish ceremonial to which that refers, but I did once go to Padstow, before Rick Stein turned it into a seafood restaurant with a village attached, for 'Obby 'Oss Day. I'd also love to see the Abbots Bromley Horn Dancers, if only because they look so distinctively weird. For years, though, folk-dancing to me meant Easter Saturday at Bacup. That was where I got my annual fix; indeed it was decades before I went to Bacup on any other day than Easter Saturday. There's not much point, really. Wikipedia describes Easter Saturday as the biggest day on Bacup's cultural calendar; it might equally well be described as the only day on Bacup's cultural calendar. In fact, it only needs a cultural egg-timer, because for 364 days a year, Bacup is a deeply unremarkable town. It has one unlikely son in Johnny Clegg, half of the South African band, Juluka, sometimes known as 'The White Zulu,' but that's just about it.

On Easter Saturday, though, Bacup is the centre of the clog-dancing universe. It is then that the Brittania Coco-Nut Dancers assemble at 9 in the morning at the Travellers' Rest on the Bacup Rochdale Road and spend the rest of the day dancing their way through the pubs and clubs of the town. Their dance - or series of dances - is unique to them, consisting of a processional element through the streets plus a garland dance and a strange little coconut dance that they perform at various fixed points, usually on licensed premises - all accompanied by members of the Stacksteads Band.

I first went to witness this spectacle in my early teens and, naturally, I thought it was fantastic. Part of the appeal, admittedly, was being able to attach yourself to the Nutters and get into pubs that were supposedly shut in those days of afternoon closing. On the contrary, they were all packed and full of music. Then the familiar lilt of the 'Tip Top Polka' would come down the street and a space would be cleared somewhere in the bar. You could be enjoying a quiet game of dominos and in would come a dozen dancers, their bandsmen and fellow-travellers. Tin trays would appear, full of halves of bitter, and the Nutters would do their world-famous Nut Dance, the unique selling point of which was the role of wooden discs on wrists and knees in beating out the tune. That could be where the coconut comes in. Or, we have to admit, it could be because the dancers are blacked-up.

Many years later, my eldest daughter and her best friend had quite an acrimonious *Guardian*-readers' argument about this, the friend insisting that it was clearly racist and the daughter equally convinced that it was nothing of the sort. Needless to say, there is no 19th century minute of an AGM when they decide to black-up because they believed that black people were inherently comical or inferior. On top of the Moorish or minstrel show or disguise themes that are advanced as explanations for black-face dancers elsewhere, there are a couple of extra ones floating around in Bacup. One is the theory that the dances and costumes came North with Cornish tin-miners, who would no doubt be as black as Welsh coal-miners by the time they finished their shift. I prefer a theory that has the advantage of a certain child-like simplicity. They do it because it matches. Their breeches, pullovers and clogs are black; the black faces fit in with that. The hat and the sort of Greek army skirt they wear is white with red and blue piping - and that forms a contrast, without meaning to mock Greek people in any way.

The strange thing is that they don't always seem to

have been blacked-up. Newsreel footage from 1930 shows them as pale as you would expect of men brought up in the Rossendale Valley, where, to quote Wikipedia again: 'Precipitation is not uncommon.' That lends weight to the theory that they copied the minstrel shows. Be that as it may, my daughter's pal won't touch it with a barge-pole. Perhaps Johnny Clegg and his Zulus of various hues would be the ideal ones to adjudicate.

I owe the Nutters a lot - possibly what passes for my career. In 1975, I was on a post-graduate journalism in Cardiff and I was in the process of screwing it up. I'd already earned a reputation for unreliability, missing a few deadlines because, quite honestly, I couldn't be bothered. They gave me a dig in the ribs to remind me that the main feature article on which we would be assessed was due in the following morning. I had done nothing about it, so I went to the pub and, when I got home, knocked out a piece about the Britannia Coco-Nut Dancers off the top of my head.

It transformed my standing and reputation. I was no longer the bone-idle slacker; I was the temperamental writer. Better still, the head of the course, Tom Hopkinson, who among many other things had been Bert Lloyd's editor at *Picture Post,* flogged it to some magazine for me. Between them, the Nutters of Bacup and the Grand Old Man of British journalism had pointed me in the right direction. There could be something in this writing caper. There could be a living to be made out of describing things that interested me. I've been getting away with it ever since.

Ten years later, Bacup almost scuppered my wedding. Attend to this cautionary tale, because this is the sort of thing that could happen to anyone. The future Mrs Wrong Steps and I spent the Saturday before our nuptials with the Coco-Nut Dancers, as you do. What I shouldn't have done was to leave my wallet on the roof of our white Mini after I paid for petrol in the town, especially when that wallet contained our marriage licence. Naturally, it fell off the roof and into the gutter at the next corner. There it was spotted and retrieved by a Bacup resident. Equally naturally, she checked the contents to see if there was anything that would help get it back to its owner. When she examined the licence, she was able, by some bizarre co-incidence, to announce: 'I know her. I was at school with her.'

From there, it was just a matter of spotting her in the crowd and returning to us what we didn't even know we had lost. If there wasn't some benevolent spirit at work among the Nutters that day, I don't know how else to explain it.

If you were to look for a justification in the 21st century for grown men to dress up and clog-dance through the streets, then I would suggest that it can be found in the reactions of children. My kids have loved it - I have their permission to say that - and now I've introduced a new generation to its delights, almost too successfully. My grandson, Ted, came to me rather apologetically after his first Easter Saturday in Bacup. 'Grandad,' he said, 'I'm not sure I want to be a professional rugby league player any more.' Actually, he said 'processional,' but you can understand his confusion. 'I want to be a Coco-nut Dancer.' To tell the truth, young man, I'd be happy with either.

In 2012, Coco-nut Dancing Day nearly didn't take place at all. Rossendale Council and the Police were demanding £1600 to finance the stewarding of the event - notoriously prone to outbreaks of mindless violence as it is. Actually, there was a bit of a scrap one year in front of the Conservative Club, so it doesn't do to be complacent about these things. The video I have which includes old footage of the Nutters carries an over 12s sticker and a warning that it contains 'dangerous activities which could be copied.' In other words, don't try this at home. Eventually, a Great British Compromise was thrashed out. One of the Nutters described the respective negotiating stances to me as follows: 'It was just the council and the police being arse-holes.'

'Careful Fred,' said a second Nutter, who had correctly identified me as just a little too curious. 'Don't forget to tell him it was all settled amicably.'

'Ah yes,' said the first Nutter, 'the arse-holes settled it amicably.'

The nature of the compromise seemed to be that there was a lot less dancing on the actual streets, necessitating less road closures. After all, the local economy - traditionally based on carpet-slippers - would grind to a halt if you could only drive unencumbered around Bacup on 364 days a year. In 2012, the Nutters merely walked between pubs, clattering into action when they arrived. It wasn't quite the same, but their clogs and coconuts will outlive Health and Safety, I'm confident of that. The future is in safe hands - or safe clogs.

Heave Away: The Irresistible Rise of the Sea Shanty and its Impact on Mental Health

I KNEW I was cracking up when I woke up one morning and couldn't face a double CD of sea shanties.

I woke up one morning - sounds like the start of a blues - but I'd been building up to it for some time. A cancer scare; a career which, it seemed to me, was going into a tail-spin after 20-odd years of onwards and upwards; stress at work; stress at home; working too hard; playing too hard. Suddenly, everything was all a bit too hard and I started to shut down. Now, I'm not claiming that this was a fully-fledged breakdown; you don't 'get over' them as quickly as I did. The friendly young Indian doctor at Heaton Medical Centre told me that I was clinically depressed. I could have told him that. For a mercifully short period of time, until the pills kicked in, I couldn't do anything. I couldn't read, I certainly couldn't write. For a few nightmarish days, I couldn't listen to music. In fact, anything I did try to listen to at that time still gives me problems today.

That's where *Rogue's Gallery* comes in. It must be the most bizarre folk concept album ever conceived; a series of shotgun weddings between unlikely songs and even more unlikely singers. How else is one to describe Bryan Ferry performing 'The Cruel Ship's Captain,' Sting's take on 'Blood Red Roses' or Nick Cave essaying 'Fire Down Below'? Weirdest of all is cartoonist Ralph Steadman cannibalising 'Little Boy Billee.' All it's short of is 'The Rambling Sailor' dragged to the yard-arm and thrashed within an inch of its life by Boy George, or Bananarama, or me ..... or all of us simultaneously. A little far-fetched, you might say, but could the results really be any odder than Ferry with Antony (of the Johnsons) hamming up *Lowlands Low*? It was a project put together by Johnny Depp (aka Captain Jack Sparrow,) who must have the income of a small country. Therefore, no-one was going to say 'no' to him, even when they knew they should. Perhaps he'd got so deeply into his role in *Pirates of the Caribbean* that he couldn't get out again. Either way, I don't recommend it during a personal melt-down. There are tracks that cling to a few vestiges of normality, like sailors clinging to a splintered and sinking lifeboat. Richard Thompson, Martin and Eliza Carthy are on it and their tracks are like coming up for air.

Now, it will have occurred to the more observant among you that not all of the songs mentioned so far are, strictly speaking, shanties. I calculate that 20 of the 43 on *Rogue's Gallery* can be described that way, if you stretch the definition to include call-and-response songs designed for singing after work rather than during it. That's enough to make it the album's dominant currency and underline what a peculiar proposition it is. I've tried to listen to it again recently, but it's like the pub bore telling a joke; it goes on forever.

Sea shanties were the rhythmic work-songs of sailing ships, made to render back-breaking jobs, like hauling up sails or turning the capstan, a little easier. As such, they could hardly be more obsolete, because the era of sail has gone and it isn't coming back. A later age, however, has found a use for them. Their practical function might have disappeared, but they still answer some sort of need. The call-and-response element that is an essential part of them is thought to go back to African work-songs. The roots of popular music do not go much deeper. Indeed, if insistent rhythm is the salient feature of most pop music, then shanties are rhythm in its purest form. They don't die out, because we keep hauling them back.

Shanties have always seemed to me to be a sort of semi-autonomous annexe to folk song. In terms of getting immersed in them, their devotees have more in common with the Sealed Knot than with a casual folk club audience. It's something to do with everyone being a performer; good grief, even I can sing along with 'The Hog's Eye Man' or 'Bully in the Alley' - to quote two of the more intriguing titles - without the ship running aground. Perhaps it is also to do with us being a supposedly maritime nation, something that permeates as far inland as Meriden in the West Midlands, which is apparently as far from the sea as you can get in England. If you think that your bog-standard folkie can be a bit of an odd sight, then your fully-fledged shantyman is really living the dream. Even if he has never been to sea, he will be a little unsteady on his pins on dry land. It's a little sub-culture within a sub-culture.

Every now and then, though, it comes out into the daylight. The Clancys had a hit in various parts of the world with 'South Australia.' Bruce Springsteen recorded 'Pay Me the Money Down' and, perhaps most fitting of all, The Sex

Pistols regaled us with 'Frigging in the Rigging.' The theme music to kids' favourite *SpongeBob SquarePants*? I'm surprised you need to ask. Sea shanty!

Even those last two words, however, have the capacity to be pulled in more than one direction. Stan Hugill, the doyen of the shanty, was insistent that they should never be called sea shanties, a shanty by definition coming from the sea. One example that puts a question mark against that is a performance from the Bright Light Quartet recorded by Alan Lomax somewhere on the eastern seaboard of America in 1960.

It's simply called 'Chantey,' employing the alternative spelling which is supposed to reflect French origins (chanter = to sing). It is also, even by shanty/chantey standards, effortlessly and jubilantly lewd.

Despite all these brushes with us landlubbers, shanties have remained resolutely separate. If you had suggested a few years ago that they would be the spearhead of an assault on the charts, you would have been dismissed as having spent too long in the crow's-nest and probably keel-hauled and made to walk the plank for good measure. But then there came ten men from out of the West to fulfil the prophesy.

Ten middle-aged men from out of Port Isaac, to be precise, because the Fisherman's Friends - named also after a particularly warming throat lozenge made in Fleetwood - grew out of singing together in the pubs of that Cornish fishing village. They put out two CDs independently, largely for the benefit of visitors who wanted a souvenir of the impromptu sessions they had heard on their visits. Word spread and the Port Isaac's Fisherman's Friends began to sing further afield. When their third album came out in 2011, it was on Universal, a mega-label if ever there was one, and it sailed straight into ninth position in the charts. Not the shanty charts, mind you; the proper job charts. That meant that thousands of people had actually gone out and bought one. With their own money. Some of them must have previously considered themselves firmly anti-shanty, but that eponymous CD - very useful, by the way, for illustrating the correct use of the apostrophe - had become an unlikely cross-over hit. It's perfectly fine. They aren't the greatest singers whom ever cleared their throats into the teeth of a brisk sou'wester, but I bet they sound fantastic in the pub, with a pint of St Austell in hand. They don't have a dominant lead singer, like a Mike Waterson or a Peter Bellamy, at the helm, but they don't need one. They hit the right note with a wider public and they did it with sea shanties, of all things.

By folk music standards, everything was going almost too well, but that was to change as suddenly as the weather off the Scillies. Whilst they were setting up at a festival in Guildford, a heavy door crashed down onto the stage, killing their manager, Paul McMullen. A few days later, one of the group, Trevor Grills, died in hospital from his injuries. It all carries a strange echo of the sort of accident that happens at sea, rather than when you are merely preparing to sing about it.

Meanwhile, a couple of hundred miles North, I'm lying on a trolley in a specialist's surgery. 'I'm Dr So-and-So,' he says. 'I do most of the bowel cancers in Bolton.'

'If that's who you are - no offence and if it's all the same to you - I'd rather be seeing someone else. I only came in to be cheered up a bit.'

He succeeded in doing that, to an extent, when, after various probes and an exploratory operation, he was able to give me the all-clear. I still felt pretty rubbish and, after a lot more tests elsewhere, it transpired that, although I didn't have the Big C, I did have the Medium-Sized P. I call it that because, bloody inconvenient though it is, Parkinson's Disease won't kill you. I've seen enough to realise that, as far as progressive neurological disorders are concerned, I've got the kind and friendly one. Besides, I'm quite relieved too that I've got a progressive disease. You wouldn't want one of those reactionary diseases, forever whinging on about foreign ailments and how they always get preferential treatment.

In view of the above procedures, I'm slightly reluctant to describe the unexpected impact of sea shanties around this time as a two-pronged attack. Waiting in the wings and gathering strength, however, were a very different ten men - or ten men and one woman - from all points of the compass. They were to draw much of their power and direction from the humble shanty.

But more of the phenomenon that is Bellowhead anon. First I have another double challenge to face, in the shape of the sequel, *Son of Rogue's Gallery*. I can only hope that they don't carry on, for generation after generation, like the *Morris On* dynasty. *Son of.....* includes - and I promise I'm not making any of these up - Tom Waits and Keith Richards singing 'Shenandoah,' Anjelica Huston's version of 'Mrs McGraw' and Iggy Pop's sensitive interpretation of 'Asshole Rules the Navy.' Something there for every mood, I would have thought. And I must be better, I think, because I positively enjoyed Ivan Neville's 'Mr Stormalong' and Macy Gray doing 'Off to Sea Once More.'

Either a lot better, or much, much worse.

A Weird and Wonderful World: Or How the Hell Did That Get There?

THEY say that you don't really know someone until you've re-arranged their CD collection. There are certain broad principles, like men filing alphabetically and women any old way; I've never cracked their code, but I think it might be something to do with colours.

As a rational human being, I start at A and go through to Z, or from Abana Ba Nasery to the Young Tradition, except that it isn't quite as simple as that. There are little colonies of music from certain related artists, particular countries (Cuba, Morocco) and, after the end of the alphabet, there are all the samplers and compilations, in any old order, as though I had got bored and delegated that part of the job to one of the women in the family. I'd still back myself to find anything when I really need it. For instance, if I fancy a bit of Kenyan skiffle-type stuff, played on guitar and Fanta bottle, I know I have to reach up to the top left corner for Abana Ba Nasery. I heard them on the radio once and liked them enough to track down their album. It has to be an old-school Fanta bottle, incidentally, because only those ridges give the right sound. I don't play the CD every day, admittedly, but I'd be that bit poorer without it.

A lunge towards the middle-right section brings us to Tavagna, and their unaccompanied polyphonic singing from Corsica - a holiday impulse purchase.

Not far away is one I can honestly say I bought purely on the strength of the name of the group - the Red Hot Chilli Pipers, whose album includes rip-roaring versions of such pillars of the bagpipe repertoire as 'Smoke on the Water,' 'Eye of the Tiger' and 'We Will Rock You.'

Then there's George Hetherington. You won't have heard his repertoire unless you've caught a particular taxi in Wellington, New Zealand. George divides his time between ferrying passengers from the airport to the city and his other life as a countryish singer-songwriter. In fact, he's found a way of combining the two. As you crawl towards the Kiwi capital, he sticks his CD on the stereo. 'Like the music?' he says. 'To you, $15.' George's unique selling point is his pricing policy. A ride into town and a CD seems to cost less than the fare on its own. It can only be a matter of time before he storms the New Zealand charts. I got the special triple offer of taxi-ride, CD and life story. Jet-lag made my retention of that third part of the deal an impossible task, but I do remember that it was tragic enough to provide him with an abundance of raw material.

Perhaps that makes this the ideal moment to introduce my all-purpose, condensed Country 'n' Western template, on which I've been working for some time. I call it 'I'll Sure Be Glad I Left You When I'm Through Being Sad You're Gone,' but that barely hints at its versatility, because every possible element is interchangeable. For I'll, read You'll;

for Glad, read Sad; for I, read You; for You, read I, and so on; and that's before you throw He, She and They into the mix. Mathematicians have calculated that, working on this principle, there are several hundred thousand variations. Some of them don't make much sense. Heck, isn't life like that, though? And all human life is there. Just imagine a late-vintage Johnny Cash running through the variations.

Apart from The Man In Black and one or two others, I've always had trouble with C&W, but not half as much as I've had with jazz. I think it goes back to my grandad pronouncing on it. 'Jazz.....' I remember him telling me, '.....some people pretend they understand it, but they don't really.' That was pretty dismissive considering that he looked more like a bandsman from New Orleans than one from New Mills. It is also a signpost to where we must go for the most unlikely album for me to be listening to as I write this; to the mysterious realm of jazz, but also to the bagpipes.

I made an effort with jazz; I've even got a couple of token Miles Davis LPs lying about somewhere, as you had to if you wanted to be cool in the 70s. I didn't really take off my shoes and socks and wade in, however, until fate decreed that my best mate in Australia should be a jazz buff. He'd always had a bit of a block with anything too folky, so when it came to that time of day when you crack open something from the Hunter Valley and stick on an album he had to delve deep into his collection to find something that might suit us both. What he came up with was *Scotch & Soul*, a mid-60s album by one Rufus Harley. He was a black American sax player, who adopted the Highland bagpipes as his primary instrument after seeing the Black Watch play at John F. Kennedy's funeral in 1963. On the album, he plays jazz standards like 'A Nightingale Sang In Berkeley Square,' in a way that appalled jazz purists. It's completely weird and really rather wonderful and any time I'm at Ian's house in Sydney it's the first thing on the turntable. Among the novices to whom Rufus gave lessons, by the way, was Muhammad Ali, before he was diagnosed with Parkinson's.

I've never found a copy of *Scotch & Soul* and I don't think it ever made it onto CD. I did, however, track down a three CD set of Rufus (!!!) entitled *Bagpipes of the World*. Actually, obscurity is no longer any barrier to bringing the weird and wonderful into your home. If it exists, Amazon can sling it in your direction. My next challenge for them will be the Malawi Mouse Boys, and I don't imagine it will take them more than a couple of days before they squeak onto the door-mat. They are a gang of street vendors, specialising in grilled rodent kebabs, who formed a gospel group. They sound terrific; listen to them sing and you can almost smell the mice sizzling on the barbecue. And that, you could argue, is pretty much the object of the exercise.

Late Onset Folkiness: An Appeal

THERE is an affliction that, even in the 2000-and-whatevers, dares not speak its name in polite company. You often hear it said that people born with a particular disability cope better than those who lose some capacity later in life. Similarly, if you're born with the folkie gene, or acquire it in your youth, then you tend to take the indignities to which you are subjected in your stride. I think you have a filter in place which takes care of most of the hey-nonny, finger in the ear treatment that you can expect from the uninitiated. Water off a dead swan's back.

But imagine living a conventional musical life for several decades and then discovering that, along with your pewter tankard, you are carrying the gene. It is on behalf of these unfortunates that I am appealing to you today.

Late-onset folkiness can take many forms, but I would ask you to reflect on two not-untypical case studies. As with so many afflictions, it can be the family and friends who really suffer. Take one of my main gig-going mates at the moment, for instance. He wants to remain anonymous, so we'll call him Keith, because that's his name. In his fifties, but loath to admit it, his idea of a great night out was, until a few years ago, to see the Who or the Stones or Paul McCartney, from half a mile away. Now he sits on the front row in pubs and arts centres to see people no-one else he knows has ever heard of. He drives around proudly with the Topic label's seven-CD boxed set belting out of the open windows. A blast of Margaret Barry at the traffic lights can cause a bit of a stir. I get e-mails from him, usually informing me of some gig which has slipped underneath my radar, signed 'From your greatest convert.....'

How did this happen? As with many potentially addictive substances, it all started with one toe dipped warily in the water. Surely that can't do any harm. But, from Spiers and Boden, you move on to the harder stuff, to Bellowhead, Oysterband, June Tabor, Martin Simpson and the Unthanks, to name some of his current favourites. And before you know where you are, you're on the midnight train home after seeing Fay Hield in a pub in Sheffield, already planning where to see her next. This is where the zeal of the convert meets the mad stare of the obsessive.

Now, don't get me wrong. I like Fay Hield. I like her and her singing very much. She's also a scholar of the music and Mrs Jon Boden. They have children and she probably dresses them in designer clothes which she makes from wool she finds on the moors. She's the renaissance woman of 21st century folk. I'm lukewarm about her, though, compared to Keith, who has something close to a teenage crush. This is the sort of thing that can happen.

Let me introduce you to another victim, my youngest daughter, Sophie. Yes, the girl with the flute on the bus, if you are reading this in chronological order. Very conveniently, she has just loomed up at my elbow whilst I'm writing this. 'I hope you're not going to write anything embarrassing about me,' she says. Sorry kiddo, but you've left me with no choice.

'I am NOT a folkie,' goes another of her pronouncements. 'I'm a young, modern person, who just happens to like a few folkie things.' Yeah, yeah - like anything to do with Bellowhead, the Unthanks and Jim Moray - especially Jim Moray. We saw him, good as he was, comprehensively played off stage by the reunion of the reggae/polka maestros, Edward II, at Buxton and she was outraged.

She remains in denial about the degree of her folkiness, but, as a clincher, let me give you one word - Ocarina. I rest my case. Mind you, Sophie's idea of cutting edge modernity is playing vinyl Bee Gees LPs on a vintage record player. It is as though I, at a similar age, had insisted on wax cylinders - a much 'warmer' sound - and a dog sitting by the ear trumpet. When Maurice Gibb, one of the high-pitched, finger in the ear brothers from the Isle of Man, died a few years ago, she was genuinely distressed and her mother asked me to have a word with her. 'I'm alright now,' she assured me. 'I was upset at the time, obviously, but then I thought of all the tribute specials on TV.' Bringing up children can be a fine balance between sentiment and practicality, but I think we got it right there.

Another regular companion at gigs is Dave. He's a folkie of half a century's standing and it isn't even his favourite music. Put a gun to his head and he would opt for bluegrass. He knows that I'm a small-doses type of punter when it comes to this particular genre, but occasionally he comes up with something that he knows I'll enjoy. There was one such gig at Wigan Parish Church recently, which he assured me wasn't all that bluegrass. He was right about that; to me, it was just standard-issue soft rock, with any punch it might have possessed lost up in the ecclesiastical rafters. Worse still, he'd brought along another chap, a bit of a purist. 'If that's bluegrass,' he said, 'I'll show my arse on the town hall steps.'

Latecomer or long-term devotee, though, you can expect to be regularly misrepresented if you get the bug for any of this music, especially if it's English folk song. It might be helpful, then, at this point, to run through a few of the calumnies to which you will be subjected, along with a few domestic veracities you can throw back at your tormentors.

1. *It all sounds the same.*

A. If, say, Bellowhead and The Unthanks, to cite two very successful current acts, sound to you like they come from the same planet, it's time to have your hearing checked. It's possible to dislike both, of course, but not for the same reasons.

2. *It's all gibberish.*

A. Not all of it. Some of it, admittedly, but you only have to buy into the principle of the chorus for it all to make perfect sense. Singing without words definitely has its place across a broad swathe of music. When Nik Cohn wrote his account of the early days of rock'n'roll - a far more heavily documented genre than this - he called it *Awopbopaloobop Alopbamboom*, quoting directly from Little Richard's 'Tutti Frutti.' When Leonard Cohen promised his audience in London in 2008 the secret meaning of life, it turned out to be 'Do dom do dom da do dom dom.'

The folk song chorus is our answer to this degree of profundity. For my money, the greatest of all choruses is from a song called 'Boston Harbour,' first popularised by The Watersons and included on the first Spiers and Boden CD. 'To me big bow-wow, Tow-row-row. Fol di row di ri do day.'

It loses a little in translation onto the printed page, but before they die everyone should have the experience of bellowing it out with a few score kindred spirits in the (preferably smoky) upstairs room of a pub. I can assure you that it makes perfect sense then. So much so that I thought of doing a Nik Cohn and calling this book *To me big bow-wow, tow-row-row.....* Maybe better not.

3. *You can't tell what it's about.*

A. Well, true, if you want a single, incontrovertible meaning for everything. A folk song has been through a lot of pairs of hands and each of them has had the chance to add an extra layer of meaning to it. It would be unnatural for it to always travel in a predictable straight line. Besides, who wants to understand absolutely everything? That's the mistake they made with the *New English Bible*. Take all the magic and mystery out and set it all down in the language of an Ikea assembly leaflet and nobody believes any of it any more.

4. *It's depressing.*

A. I think we've dealt with that one already.

5 *It's irrelevant to the modern world.*

A. It might be, if the basics of human life had changed all that much. There's as much of what we now call dysfunctional behaviour - everything from rape, abduction, murder, incest, necrophilia, suicide (with or without pacts) and paedophilia to more surreal and psychedelic stuff like spirit possession, talking animals, shape-changing and rising from the dead (often with a jolly chorus attached) - in a random dip into the folk song canon as there is in ten episodes of *The Jeremy Kyle Show*. If that's irrelevance, it's a very lively form of it.

5. *It feeds into a cultural nationalism that can turn into xenophobia.*

A. Now this is one that really hurts, because it runs so directly counter to what we think we are about. When Nick Griffin tried to co-opt the music of Eliza Carthy, among others, for his horrible agenda, it caused a sick feeling in the collective stomach. The historic politics of the various folk revivals has always been of the left; you could mortally insult anyone by calling them a Tory, never mind a member of the BNP. Artists who feared they might be linked with the organisation were quick to dissociate themselves from it and all its works. It could still do damage, because you have to have some knowledge of the scene to know how bogus the link is.

The best defence is the music that comes out of it. Far from excluding outside influences, English folk in the 21st century positively reaches out and grabs them. If anything should give Griffin nightmares, it is surely The Imagined Village, with their cross-fertilisation of bolshie Brits (the Carthys, Chris Wood, Billy Bragg) and Asian percussion and sitar. You can further point out that the best description of the politics of folk music is the singer Roy Bailey's contention that it is the common man's version of history.

Tell them that. They'll probably still stick their fingers in their ears, but tell them anyway.

Muck and Brass: How Bellowhead Saved My Life

Not a chapter heading to be taken too literally, surely. Bands, even genre-busting 11-strong folk bands, do not save lives.

In this case, though, they just might have done. There are snipers all over this green and pleasant land with orders to shoot me if they ever hear me drone on about the good old days, about how much better things were when I was a lad; if I turn into an old fogey, as well as an old folkie, in other words. The same contract applies to other subjects as well, like rugby and beer and literature and politics. Any one of them might land me in the cross-hairs of a high-powered rifle, because, let's face it, sometimes things were better in the past. One day, I might be boring someone to death about it, when there will be a distant 'crack' and I'll never bore anyone ever again.

I think I'm fairly safe from it being folk music that triggers the hit, because I firmly believe that there is more great music around than ever. And top of the tree are the best, the most enjoyable and perhaps the most significant performers I've heard in 50 years.

The roots of Bellowhead lie in the collaboration between Jon Boden (fiddle, guitar and vocals) and John Spiers (squeezeboxes) that became the most popular duo on the folk scene. You could compare them to Carthy and Swarbrick or The Dransfields in their particular eras, the difference being that they always felt and sounded like a MUCH bigger band trying to get out. Apparently, they used to wile away the hours in traffic jams going to and from gigs playing a game that might have been called Fantasy Band Members. By the time they founded Bellowhead, they were up to ten; the tuba player, Gideon Juckes, joined a little later. Had they been stuck in a tailback on the M6 for long enough, they could have been as big as the Mormon Tabernacle choir.

I already had S&B pencilled in for a special role in my musical destiny from the moment I discovered that the first track on their first CD, *Through and Through*, was none other than our old shipmate, 'The Rambling Sailor.' Not only that, it was the most rip-roaring, rollicking, confident version ever recorded up to that time; live, it was even better. In other words, it was as far removed from me, squirming and sweating under the spotlight at the Balmoral Hotel, as it was possible to be.

In his sleeve notes, Boden describes the song's 'commission from the queen to court all girls [as] is handsome' as 'one of the lesser- known royal appointments,' although Japan, it should be noted, has a minister for population increase, which is not a million miles away.

'Moralists may take comfort from the fact that the protagonist gets his comeuppance - albeit in a different version of the song [see "Trim Rigged Doxy"].'

Or to put it another way, the clap he so richly

deserves. Boden attributes his version to Maddy Prior's one-time partner, Tim Hart.

S&B would have done nicely for me if they had never gone beyond being the world's best twosome. Like master criminals putting together a team of all the talents for one big heist, though, they had more ambitious plans. The Bellowhead sound would be built around the fiddle of Boden and the melodeon of Spiers, but with so much more going on at the same time. There would be a maximum of three other fiddles, doubling as cello, oboe and bagpipes. There would be the almost impossibly inventive percussion of Pete Flood, plus the plethora of plucked strings from Benji Kirkpatrick - son of John, who we first met several chapters ago in rural Shropshire.

Already, they are shaping up as a pretty damn unusual folk band. Their defining feature, though, is the prominence of a four-man brass section.

Considering that they co-exist in a lot of the same communities, folk music types and brass (or silver) bands have tended to keep each other at a wary arm's length. Them in their flannels and blazers up that end of the village; us in our jeans and sweaters at the other. There were exceptions, like the Coco-nut Dancers, every Easter Saturday at Bacup, but by-and-large the two went their own ways. There was always a bit of an unspoken attraction there, however, and Bellowhead were by no means the first to try to bring them together.

Not only was Richard and Linda Thompson's 'I Want to See the Bright Lights Tonight' the great folk cross-over hit that never happened, it also featured the CWS Band, lending the whole thing an irresistible poignancy.

The same goes for Roy Harper's 'When an Old Cricketer Leaves the Crease,' that track to which I strode out confidently to bat in the cricket match to celebrate my 60th birthday and, a couple of verses later, strode back. Rumour has it that this was the track John Peel wanted to be played at his funeral, but he had to settle for 'Teenage Kicks' by the Undertones.

Then there are the bands that have built their whole approach around the interplay between the blare of brass and more conventional folk instruments. We haven't spent as much time as we ought to have in Quebec so far, but we must hie there immediately to accord full recognition to La Bottine Souriante, which translates rather clumsily as The Smiling Boot and has connotations of being down-at-heel. There is nothing down-at-heel about LBS's music, though. It's a glorious, stomping wall of sound, like cajun, but even better, with trombones and saxophones fighting it out with fiddles, squeezeboxes and percussive feet. I've only seen them once, at a free concert in front of Bradford Town Hall, of all places, but their CDs play an important role in the rhythm of my working days. I call it deadline music, because I've found nothing that goes as well with trying to type quickly. Just writing about them now has put an extra ten words-per-minute on my normally sluggish rate of progress.

Back in Britain, other pioneers of brass included The Home Service. Originally an off-shoot of Ashley Hutchings's Albion Band, they carved out their own distinctive style, with a rock front-line and a rather classically-nuanced brass section. They re-formed in 2013 and their sold-out reunion gigs were some of the best of the year.

Then, out on their own, there is Brass Monkey - the clue is in the name - which is essentially Messrs Carthy and Kirkpatrick (Snr) plus a brass section. They have been an on-and-off sort of proposition for the best part of 30 years, but, whenever they have been gigging, they have made a quite glorious noise. I once arrived a couple of hours early for one of their re-union gigs in a pub in Manchester and they were quite happy to let me in for the sound-check. In this case, that was a bit of a misnomer, because they were not so much checking the sound as re-learning their old repertoire and trying out some old stuff. It was fizzing and flying about in all directions and sounded at times like half a dozen musicians playing different tunes, but then the show proper started and, wham, it was just like they'd never been away.

Bellowhead have always acknowledged their debt to them; without Brass Monkey, there could have been no Bellowhead.

There are others, though, at what might be termed the younger end of the spectrum who have picked up the brass theme and run with it.

Sam Lee is one of the most distinctive interpreters of English folk song and his typical accompaniment tends to be something along the lines of banjo, trumpet and Jew's harp. Hands up if you spotted that combination coming down the track; surely room, you would have thought, for an ocarina in there somewhere.

The most spectacular collaboration between folk and brass, however, has to be via The Unthanks. The girls from the North East and their entourage are a perfect example of the restless energy and the search for new directions of some of the best folk acts. They could have continued to make a living doing what they did on their first few albums, when they were Rachel Unthank and the Winterset - Unthank, incidentally, being a not-uncommon surname in their part of rural Northumbria, rather than a piece of Orwellian Newspeak. Not for them a comfy niche in the status quo, though. Not only have they expanded the range of their main repertoire, they have also embarked on a series of fascinating side-projects, like the music of Antony and the Johnsons and Robert Wyatt or the history of shipbuilding. Most cherished of all by those lucky enough to see them, however, have been their concerts with the Brighouse and Rastrick Band, who are not merely the most celebrated in Britain, but in Yorkshire too. I have already described the effect their rendition of 'The King of Rome' can have on the unwary. A full concert of The Unthanks at their most ethereal, accompanied by the sort of moody brass that sold a billion loaves of Hovis can turn the most militant anti-folkie into a tankard-carrying fellow-traveller.

What Bellowhead do with a brass section is something different again. The first thing you have to understand about them is that they are LOUD. Even the songs and tunes that start relatively quietly have a habit of getting louder and louder. The main factor in this is the 'oomph' given to their music by the combination of trumpet, trombone, saxophone and heliotron - a sort of tuba for the 21st century that now provides the bass layer. Faced with that potentially overwhelming fire-power, playing away quietly elsewhere on stage is not an option.

Another sense in which brass sections seem to set the pace, in all forms of music in which they get involved, is that they are famous for being the thirstiest of musicians. It must be all that breath control. I once had the pleasure and privilege of directing Bellowhead's brass section to the best real ale pub in Ludlow, when they were in danger of wasting precious drinking time. It doesn't quite make me an honorary band member, but I was happy to help out.

If the horns power Bellowhead's sound, there is no real dispute about the single dominant personality in the band. It has come as a surprise to me to find that not everybody likes Jon Boden and the way he goes about running the show. For one thing, he hogs all the lead vocals; but then again he is incomparably the best singer in the band. Or he is to me, at any rate. I've argued with others for whom he is just too strident, too theatrical, too declamatory; just too much of everything, really. Whilst respecting everybody's views in this matter, that really is bollocks. If ever a band needed a strong central figure to hold it together, it is Bellowhead. Boden is it and, as such, he is the one member who is irreplaceable. Where he does run a risk is in trying to do too much.

Not only is he the focal point of the leading folk and roots band in Britain, he also has an offshoot band called The Remnant Kings, whose repertoire includes powerful material that he wrote for his solo albums. He still works as a hugely popular duo with John Spiers. He has worked in his wife, Fay Hield's band, The Hurricane Party, and he is the go-to man as a session musician on fiddle.

Just in case all this left him twiddling his thumbs in frustrated inactivity, he embarked a couple of summers ago on the sort of project that could eat up what remains of your life in one mighty swallow. In *A Folk Song a Day* he recorded a different song for every day of the year and released them through the internet. No waking up on November 28 with little Bodens running around the house, feeling a bit grotty and not bothering. Folk Song is a hard taskmaster and the new track has to be there. Not only did it become a morning ritual for a lot of very strange people like me - brush teeth, folk song, coffee - but it now forms a massive archive of songs, 365 of them, to be precise, which he is inviting others to share. It's another reason why I put Jon Boden in the Mt Rushmore of giants of English folk music, alongside Bert Lloyd, Ewan MacColl, Martin Carthy, Peter Bellamy and Nic Jones. These, to me, are the big beasts of the folk song revival.

You could argue that, in terms of sheer range and variety of work, Nic Jones is lucky to qualify to be hewn out of the hillside with the others, but he surely would have done all manner of other things if he had not spent the best part of 30 years recovering from his car crash and his influence is still everywhere. Likewise, the suicide at a relatively young age of Peter Bellamy. He had 'only' founded the Young Tradition, written 'The Transports' and reclaimed Rudyard Kipling for a modern audience. What else would he have achieved by now? He deserves to be there, but so does his greatest modern admirer, the boy Boden.

For all the wide range of work he has done elsewhere, it is for launching Bellowhead that I will be eternally grateful to him. I know I am safe from that particular bullet which might have had my name on it, because I can put my hand on my heart and say that they are the best thing to have happened to English folk music since ..... well, since when? Since Cecil Sharp, if we really want to get silly about it. And at the centre of it all is Jon Boden. The attitude is his; the repertoire is largely his too, gleaned from Forest Camp Schools, old LPs, sessions in pubs in Oxford and anywhere else that good material could be hiding. Just to confirm that they have got my number, what is the opening track on the first Bellowhead recording, *Eponymous*? Yep, that's right, The *Rambling Sailor*, what else, given the full, big-band treatment and preparing the way for everything that has followed.

A word about the Bellowhead song-book, because there are a couple of threads without which it would not hang together. One is the continuing love affair with the sea shanty. If Bellowhead are the world's best party band - and I would take some convincing that they are not - then shanties are the world's best party music. Their first full-length album, *Burlesque*, not only includes the well-known 'Fire Marengo,' but also 'Across the Line,' which they think combines an Australian shanty's words with a Brazilian tune. Subsequent recordings have included 'Haul Away,' 'Roll Her Down the Bay' and their favourite opening song, 'Whiskey is the Life of Man,' from *Matachin*, 'New York Girls' and the thrash-punk version of 'Little Sally Racket' on *Hedonism* and 'Roll the Woodpile Down,' which is one of the highlights of *Broadside*.

Another of the nautical strands that runs through their work could be bracketed as Sailors and Whores; like Doctors and Nurses, but folkier. It's a popular subject in folk song, but not as popular with many as it is with Bellowhead. Their first, fully-fledged show-stopper was 'London Town,' which the fiddle and oboe player, Paul Sartin, described on stage as being 'autobiographical in the case of at least two members of the band.' (One up for the Sailor). Then there's 'The Rambling Sailor,' of course (2-0 to the Sailor), 'Yarmouth Town,' 'Go My Way' and 'Little Sally Racket.' (Late equaliser, extra time and penalties). If you count 'New York Girls' in this category - controversial late winner to the Ladies of the Night. 'You have to get up early to be smarter than a whore,' as Boden sings.

This is not the folk song canon collected and protected by Cecil Sharp and Co. These are the songs his source singers would have been too embarrassed to perform in front of a gent and a vicar. Even had they done so, he would not have passed them on in anything but the most bowdlerised form. They are the folk songs that survived the Victorian folk song revival; the mucky little cousins of the well-scrubbed ones sung around the piano.

Nor is there anything remotely politically correct about them. They are bawdy and randy and gleefully exploitative. What's not to love?

Well, that might be one of the things that makes some people a little queasy about Bellowhead and the image of England they are pumping out. Likewise, their obvious love of dressing up; to me and their audience it's all part of the fun, but what would Ewan MacColl have said, let alone Cecil Sharp?

There's only one way to judge whether it works and that is to see them live. Magnificent as their CDs are, they only give a clue to the potency of the whole Bellowhead experience. Their most breathless reviews are the ones that flag them up as the best live act in Britain, the best in the world, the best since The Who.

It took me a while to track them down and I've now seen them so often that I can't remember where we were the first time. Bury, perhaps, or Southport. What I do remember, though, is being transported, from the first notes - the brass riff of 'Prickle-Eye Bush' - to the last echoes of the third encore. Everything was spot-on, up to and including the way that, before those echoes had died down, three members of the band were in position on the merchandise stall to catch even the quickest punters on their way out.

The merchandise stall is as important a part of the folk music economy as the folk club raffle. Its prime function is to sell CDs of the acts you have just seen and, for a lot of those acts, they must be the main market-place. Such is the case of the format that you have to be pretty low in the folk pecking order not to have a CD available, usually at a nice, round £10. I remember Dave Burland recounting a conversation with his grandson.

'If they really like you, will they buy CDs?' the boy asked him. 'Well, yes, they probably will.'

'Ladies and gentlemen, don't make me a liar to my grandson.....'

Oddly enough, the place I've been to which was most swamped by home-made CDs was supposedly strictly non-entrepreneurial Cuba. You'd only had to sit down there for a beer, or a coffee and a cigar, and music would mysteriously strike up. Not only that, but within minutes the musicians would be circulating among you, flogging their CDs at $5US. You had to be a hard man to turn them down; hence a disproportionately large Cuban section in my CD racks.

Bellowhead had one problem when it came to flogging their albums. Part of the attraction is that they should be signed, but try getting 11 autographs on one CD at one time; it's a musical Labour of Hercules.

That isn't the only logistical problem that comes with being Bellowhead. To begin with, you're splitting your earnings - which, despite the comparisons, do not yet rival those of The Who - 11 ways. Then there are the complications of availability. All 11 members are members of something else as well; sometimes, as in the case of Jon Boden, of just about everything else. There is even a CD - available from the trestle table at the back of the hall - devoted to their other projects. *Umbrellowhead* includes the likes of Setsuman Bean Unit, a Japanese band involving three members of Bellowhead, and Paul Sartin's arrangement of *Psalm 143*, sung by the choir of Christ Church Cathedral, Dublin. Don't put all your eggs in one basket, lads; it might not last.

In their early days, that gave them a rather fluid line-up, with a network of deputies ready to be drafted in as back-up if some-one was pre-booked elsewhere.

One of the best Bellowhead gigs I've ever seen was at the Shrewsbury Festival with daughters two to three, inclusive. We somehow got to the front of the giant marquee, from where we could see that something wasn't quite right. It should have been virtually a home gig for Benji

Kirkpatrick, but there was a sub on deck for him and it transpired that he was previously committed to playing elsewhere that night as a duo with his dad, John. I've seen them with just about all their regulars missing at various times; except Boden, of course.

As they have become more and more successful, that has happened less frequently. For all their other activities, just about every member has Bellowhead as their main priority. And why wouldn't they? They headline festivals, get on mainstream radio and sell CDs by the trestle table-ful. When their fourth album *Broadside* came out, it went straight into the album charts at number 16 - the same spot previously kept warm by the Port Isaac's Fisherman's Friends - and number one in the independent album charts.

This is heady stuff for music nobody is interested in and it has been achieved without watering down what made them different in the first place. I'm even reassured by the occasional track I don't much like - 'The Widow's Curse' or 'Black Beetle Pies' for instance - because they make me feel as though I'm retaining some autonomy.

I do have to see them at every opportunity, though, which has twice meant turning out twice in three nights and once in successive performances. How can that be worth it, people ask. Well, seeing them with my boozing mates is an entirely different experience from taking one or more daughters. Besides, the show is always at least slightly different. I once returned in triumph from one of my double-headers with the exciting news that two songs had been in a different order. They will continue to expand their repertoire, continue to keep it fresh. I'm trying to persuade them to do a version of Leonard Cohen's 'Closing Time' - surely a strong candidate for the compulsory partly out-of-tune track on some future album - but, so far, no dice.

Even without that particular number, Bellowhead must be close to the point where they have their own tribute band, possibly featuring some of their deputies. I've even got a name for it - Below Head. They can have that for nothing, as a personal thank-you for so many great nights.

I mean the sort of night where you can bellow out 'The Rambling Sailor' or any of its successors on their play-list and no one can tell whether you're doing it competently or not. I've even trained my tremor to keep time with some of the more familiar sets of tunes, like 'The Rochdale Coconut Dance' - one that died when Bacup carried on - or 'Sloe Gin.' If I'm not quite shaking my stuff in precisely the same tempo as everyone else, the worst they will think of me is that the old, beardy bloke with the pretty daughters is finding some intricate time-signatures in the mix.

The next to the last time I saw Bellowhead was in Liverpool, where the local baddies lived down to their city's unfortunate reputation by stealing their lap-tops from the dressing rooms during the first half. Also during that first half, I became aware of more high-pitched shrieking and screaming than I am used to at a folk gig. There were about 20 mid-teenaged schoolgirls behind us and they were loving every minute of it, singing along like fury and not, as far as I'm aware, celebrating their new lap-tops. I found out from a couple of them how they came to be there. They were from the Wirral Girls Grammar School and their teacher was a huge Bellowhead fan. He had arranged it all, sound-check, meeting the band and the whole thing. I would have been equally impressed if they had been from a comprehensive in Toxteth, but you can't have everything. At the end, I sought out their teacher.

'Yes,' he admitted warily, he was in charge of them, and he prepared himself for the inevitable complaint.

'Well, I just wanted to say what a pleasure it's been hearing them enjoying it so much.'

I almost added something along the lines of: 'You know, young people today often get a bad press.....'

I heard the snipers removing their safety catches and just managed to stop myself.

End

Also by Dave Hadfield

■ Foreword by Brian Carney

Dave Hadfield's seventh book about rugby league is devoted to one of the sport's great untold stories.

Learning Curve: The Remarkable Story of Student RL tells of how Oxford and Cambridge were conquered - places the sceptics said the game would never reach. It covers the development of 13-a-side rugby in the universities of England, Wales, Scotland and Ireland, as well as Australia, France and New Zealand. Student World Cups, Ashes series and thriving domestic comps are also featured, along with the author's inimitable and witty observations on the state of play today.

From dozens of interviews with those most closely involved, league's best-loved writer captures the spirit and dedication of the elite level, plus the humour of the lower echelons. Whether you played at university or college or not, *Learning Curve* is an unmissable treat for those who care about the future of rugby league.

Call: 0113 225 9797
or to order online visit:
www.scratchingshedpublishing.co.uk